Say No, Say Yes to Change

SAY NO, SAY YES TO CHANGE

Elaine Dickson

BROADMAN PRESS
Nashville, Tennessee

© Copyright 1982 • Broadman Press
All rights reserved.
4252-10
ISBN: 0-8054-5210-9
Dewey Decimal Classification: 303.4
Subject Heading: SOCIAL CHANGE
Library of Congress Catalog Card Number:81-067375

This book is the text for a course in the subject area Christian Growth and Service of the Church Study Course.

Unless otherwise noted, Scripture quotations are from the King James Version of the Bible.

Scripture quotations marked (NEB) are from *The New English* Bible. Copyright © The Delegates of the Oxford University Press and the Syndics of the Cambridge University Press, 1961, 1970. Reprinted by permission.

Scripture quotations marked (Phillips) are reprinted with permission of Macmillan Publishing Co., Inc. from J. B. Phillips: *The New Testament in Modern English*, Revised Edition. © J. B. Phillips 1958, 1960, 1972.

Scripture quotations marked (RSV) are from the Revised Standard Version of the Bible, copyrighted 1946, 1952, © 1971, 1973.

Scripture quotations marked (TLB) are taken from *The Living Bible*. Copyright © Tyndale House Publishers, Wheaton, Illinois, 1971. Used by permission.

Expressions of Gratitude

Over the past several years, persons in training sessions I have conducted have asked, "When are you going to write a book?" This question helped keep alive my dream, initially, and then my commitment to write this book. I am especially grateful for the encouragement to put my ideas in written form which came from Allen W. Graves, Johnnie Godwin, and Steve Bond.

Friends whose professional competency I highly respect have read drafts of my manuscript and interacted with me about my ideas—questioning them, affirming them, sharpening them. I am especially grateful for this kind of interaction with Anne Davis, Doug Anderson, Robert Dean, and Trudy Tharpe. Louise Scott read my manuscript and made suggestions to improve its clarity. Gene Chamberlain, a gifted coworker literally gave me writing lessons, patiently assisting me with feedback as the manuscript developed. Billie Pate both consulted with me and gave me permission to use some of her poetic prayers to introduce each chapter—an addition which enhances the meaning of the book for me and for readers. For all these generous gifts of friendship, I am grateful.

ELAINE DICKSON

Contents

1

Lord,
Keep me from making daily
*   payments to the past*
And from prepaying some future fantasy.
Help me know I am debt free today
To spend my gifts of choice
Saying yes to life
*   . . . or sometimes no*
If no is a better way.

             —Billie Pate[1]

1

No and Yes

I backed across the smooth surface of my kitchen floor with hands outstretched. Rhythmically I called out instructions to a friend following me.

"Bend. Small. Bend. Small."

A thirty-year-old was learning to walk without a cane. Her body was saying no to walking; her will was saying yes. The "bend" was a reminder for her to get into the habit of bending her knee and lifting her foot in taking a step rather than dragging her foot along as dead weight. The "small" was a reminder to keep her steps small because her balance was so easily disturbed.

At first she took two steps before the wobbling grasp for support occurred. Then three. Then more. Walking unassisted—even a few steps—was but one of hundreds of changes Carol had experienced in the last decade of her life.

An automobile accident in 1973 changed Carol from a dramatically beautiful, confident, and poised young woman into a full-grown, sleeping baby. For six months she lay in a coma, completely dependent on caring persons around her—literally sustained in life again by her family and a mother's love expressed daily at her bedside.

One day, when hope was running out, Carol moved one finger. Change. Slowly she moved through the endless process of relearning everything she had learned earlier in life. Gaining control of body functions. Coordinating physical movement. Crawling. Talking. Writing. Walking. Gain-

SAY NO, SAY YES TO CHANGE

ing independence. Rebuilding adult relationships. And, as if all this were not enough, adjusting to divorce from her young husband when he could no longer deal with the frustration he felt in being married to a "dependent stranger." Carol was not the person he married.

Carol has an indomitable spirit. She has had to struggle repeatedly with the question, Is life worth living? Saying yes over and over again when it would have been easier to say no has given her inner strength and beauty.

Carol's life is a living testimony to her faith and hope, and these express themselves in action. Recently, in helping Carol's Aunt Billie (Billie Pate who wrote the prayers which begin each chapter in this book) prepare an amended tax return for Carol, I felt warm tears roll down my face as I added up check after check Carol had written to her church—including a check to the Lottie Moon Christmas Offering for Foreign Missions—during a year when she was struggling to live independently as a handicapped person on a six-thousand-dollar income. Almost 20 percent of her meager income had been given to her church. I touched the checks reverently because I knew they were not payments grudgingly given, but spontaneous expressions of generous gratitude for the gift of life.

Recently in my home I sat across the room from Carol. Looking up from a magazine I discovered her in a relaxed, serene posture—deep in her own private world. It was the first time I had seen so much of the "old Carol" back again. It was like discovering her for the first time. Beauty. Poise. Head erect and confident. No longer a young woman whose conversation was punctuated with giggles betraying her lack of confidence in an adult world. Perhaps she was reflecting on her current goal to complete college, anticipating her third term as a student since the accident occurred. Perhaps she was reflecting on her visit last night with a young couple and their baby, friends from college before the accident. I will never know what was in her private world. I saw the outer manifestations of purpose, peace, and joy.

I retreated to the private world of my own thoughts. Some of Paul's words about his own experiences with change came to my mind. "I have learned how to get along happily whether I have little or much. I know how to live on almost nothing or with everything. I have learned the secret of contentment in almost every situation . . . for I can do everything God asks me to with the help of Christ who gives me the strength and power. But even so, you have done right in helping me" (Phil. 4:11-14, TLB).

Then I found myself praying: *Lord, help me deal with the changes in my own life with as much assurance as Carol that you are working with me to make something good out of what happens in my life.*

Some of the changes in my life appear small compared to Carol's, but they are very important to me. Like you, I have had to deal with changes which brought me the joy of newness and the sorrow of loss, the dawn of hope and the night of despair.

While growing up, I plagued my parents with why questions. My whys were curious and spontaneous. They also were sometimes difficult to answer. They still are! But several years ago I became seriously interested in the change processes I and others were experiencing. Instead of spending so much time with Why? I started probing the What? and How? of change. And, like others who have walked into the unknown as an explorer, I return to extend to you my hand and a little light, as together we continue life's quest.

This book is for people who care for children, who work at jobs, who shop for groceries, and who mow lawns. Change affects everybody. Saying yes and no to change is something we all do daily. Whether we are aware it is happening, change occurs in our lives. Sometimes we choose change. Sometimes it is a disturbing intruder, leaving us only with the choice of how we will respond to it. We bump into change points personally, and we experience them in our relationships with husband or wife, brother and sister, friends and neighbors. Even our Christian experience is

SAY NO, SAY YES TO CHANGE

marked by continuing change—*new* life in Christ.

If you have ever had any of the following experiences, this book is for you:

Have you ever had a deep, deep longing for a change in some condition of your life but couldn't find a first step to take in making the change or you couldn't get the courage to take that step?

Have you experienced the shock of having a single event drastically change your whole life, leaving you with a stinging feeling of loss?

Have you ever seen people and situations around you changing and felt panic because your deepest desire was to keep things exactly the way they were?

Have you ever felt the overpowering joy of finally getting the courage to tell a trusted friend about something new you are considering doing and having the person say, "I believe you can!"?

Have you ever felt uncomfortable, even threatened by a new person who entered your world and seemed very different from you—uncomfortable to the extent you felt you must defend yourself from being changed by this person?

Have you ever watched a child in your life change before your very eyes and felt a strange mixture of feelings of joy and sorrow, hope and fear about what was happening?

Have you ever taken a position for or against something new and found yourself in painful, almost unbearable conflict over this with someone important to you?

Have you ever felt the frustration of knowing deep in your heart that some new course of action was right but you did nothing about it because you could not face the possible consequences of change?

To be so much a part of our everyday lives, change is a process with much unsolved mystery. No one can say precisely how or why or under what conditions we change. Change processes are individual and unique for each of us. We can say only that our experiences with change contain some common elements, forces, and dynamics which all of us experience to a greater or lesser degree, in one form or another. Our experience-in-common gives us a basis for exploring together the question of this book: What happens to us as we say no and yes to change?

- How do we react when changes are introduced into our lives?
- What forces work for and against change?
- How do we cope with both the threat and the possibility of change?
- How do we deal with the natural resistance we feel to many changes?
- What are the conditions that make it easier for us to change?
- How do we make change a natural part of our lives?
- How do we relate to persons different from us whose very presence in our lives invites or demands us to change?
- How can we manage the conflict we often experience within ourselves and between ourselves and others in change?

This book does not suggest specific changes for us to make. It is about the process of changing. This book does not deal with change on a big scale, like the changing number of old people in our population or the changing amount of energy resources in our world. The emphasis of the book is on personal change in settings, such as home, school, church, and work, where we have the possibility of person-to-person contact and face-to-face communication with other people. Massive social change, like the changing role of women, is dealt with only as it enters the smaller world of our personal experiences. This book may not help you and me change *the world*, but it should help us change and respond to change in *our world*—that part of the world we touch and which touches us.

Our lives are living monuments to the changes to which we have said yes and no and to how the yeses and nos have been said. My deepest hope is that we will be better equipped with understandings and skills to live out the advice of the apostle Paul to the Christians at Rome.

"Don't let the world around you squeeze you into its own mould, but let God re-mould your minds from within, so that you may prove in practice that the Plan of God for you is good, meets all His demands and moves toward the goal of true maturity" (Rom. 12:2, Phillips). In this passage, we are called on to say no and yes to change—to resist changes which squeeze us into the world's mold and to accept changes in harmony with God's intention. For the Christian, the ultimate objective of change is true Christian maturity. With such a worthy objective, we cannot afford to leave change to chance.

For Your Reflection

1. Recall some specific instances when you experienced one or more of the following and how you felt at the time:
   (1) A single event happened which dramatically changed your whole life.
   (2) You longed for change in the condition of your life, but couldn't find a way to change things.
   (3) You saw people and situations around you changing but your deepest desire was to keep things exactly the way they were.
   (4) A child changed before your very eyes and you were suddenly aware of the change.
   (5) A new person entered your life very different from you, and you could not ignore the difference because you feared the difference might change you.
   (6) You took a position for or against something new and got into conflict with another person(s) important to you.
   (7) You felt some new course of action was right, but you could not get the courage to do anything about it.

2. What do you hope to gain from reading this book? Does what you need or want appear to be in line with the objective of this book? Do you need to change your expectations of the book?

2

Lord,
my hope-shaped expectations for tomorrow
  are far more than a denial of today.
They give deeper meaning
  to what I know about yesterday.
And they free me to live today
  as the new time it is.

—Billie Pate

2
Walking on a Shifting Earth

Coffee break conversation started with the question, "Elaine, what are you doing these days?"

"I'm writing a book on change, of all things," was my comment. This broke open the conversation.

Andy picked up the subject immediately. "I'm experiencing change right now," he said. "I took my oldest son to college last weekend. This change was one I thought I was prepared for, but about fifty miles into my trip back home to Nashville it hit me. It's been painful ever since."

This father went on to explain, "Mark and I are close. I miss having him around. I miss the affectionate hugs which started when he was a child and later became 'bear hugs' from a six-foot, two-hundred-pound young man. I still listen for him to come in at night.

"This experience has caused me to reflect on other changes in my life," Andy shared. "This is number three on my list of 'most traumatic changes' I have ever experienced. Number one was my father's death ten years ago. Number two happened when I was in the army. My wife accompanied me to Maryland, both of us knowing she would have to return to our home in Oklahoma after three months. The day I had to put her on the bus to go home was one of the really low days cf my whole life. Now this—my oldest son leaving home."

With real insight, Andy talked on, "Maybe the changes I rank number one, two, and three are not where other people would put them, but this is my experience."

This father went on to point out that his son is very happy at college and that he, as a father, is happy for him. He also mentioned that this experience had made him even more aware of the presence of his fourteen-year-old son. They had done something together the night before they might not have done when the older son was at home. Positive possibilities were emerging in the midst of change, but this did not erase the sense of loss he felt.

Another person at coffee break with us joined in. Ralph said, "Exactly thirty-one years ago today I married and gave up my life alone for life in the new family Sue and I established. A few years ago my wife died, but family members and I were still together. Now, thirty-one years later—to the day—my youngest daughter leaves for college. This completes the cycle for me—alone, with family, alone. Change."

The earth shifts as we walk on it.

A fellow worker and I attended a seminar on "Using Time More Effectively." A week later he commented, "My formal education was completed long ago, and I have worked hard to keep learning and to apply what I know. When I went to the training session last week, I was unsure about giving a day of my time to it, but I hoped it would be profitable. Incredible! That day was one of the greatest learning experiences of my whole life. I will never be the same again, nor will I do my work exactly the same again." For this person the possibility of change based on learning was exhilarating.

Another friend lamented to me, "I hope I never have another six months like the ones just passed. I have changed jobs, moved to a new house, had illness in my immediate family, and lost my father in an automobile accident. There have been times when I didn't think I could make it another day. Some days I am still not sure." For this person the cumulative amount of change—invited and uninvited—was a burden almost too heavy to bear.

Life is change—chosen by us or forced on us. The

earth does shift as we walk on it. New conditions are being established regularly in our lives. Something new is being exchanged for something old. Shifts in direction are occurring. Something looks different than before. One thing is laid aside, abandoned, for something else. Something is lost. Something is gained. Change may range from a slight difference in what now exists to a complete transformation. Our lives keep changing.

Edward Lindaman points out, "One of the most delightful and important miracles of life occurs in the subtle merging of the person 'I am now' with the 'person not yet.' This is the miracle of being stretched—stretched to being 'more than I am.' "[1] But most of us are quick to point out that the very changes which have the possibility of making us *more* than we are threaten us with the alternative possibility of making us *less* than we are.

To Live Is to Change

Life is a mix of the old and the new, the stable and the dynamic, the changing and the changeless. The changes we experience are sometimes pluses—a new hobby, a promotion, Christian conversion. At other times the minus sign dominates—a hurricane destroys a house, illness takes a life, a wife divorces her husband, a boss fires an employee, a once functional skill becomes obsolete because of new technology.

Think about some of the major changes which have taken place in your own life during the past year. Choose from the following list as a starter and add to it: moved to a new location, became a Christian, lost someone in death, a new baby arrived, learned a new skill, lost valued property through fire or theft, joined a new organization, lost a job, changed churches, last child left home, retired from a job, made new friends, gained or lost weight, started family worship, changed financial status, changed sleeping patterns, changed health condition.

Change has always been a natural part of human growth, firmly established in the life cycle which begins before birth and ends at death. The expectation of growing and changing is built into basic life processes. As we move through ages and stages of life, we constantly move toward something new, fulfilling God's blueprint for human life. Life is a process of becoming, and becoming requires change.

Changing as a baby to become a person who not only gestures and gurgles but also crawls, walks, and talks, activating a wider use of the senses.

Changing as a child to become a person capable of exercising choice and will.

Changing as an adolescent to become a person who experiences a more complete sense of autonomy, identity, and unique worth.

Changing as an adult to become a person capable of joining life with another person to reproduce life and joining life with others to create new quality of life for humankind.

Changing throughout the life span in our awareness of and response to God, the Source of life.

Changes in our lives brought about by positive growth add to our resources for living. We develop stronger bodies, minds, and spirits. We increase our knowledge and skill. We broaden our experience and increase our capacity to deal with life.

Not only do our personal situations change but so do our group experiences with others. We change in relationship to and with other people. While the family is the primary group in which change occurs, the church, the school, and the work setting are examples of other groups in which change occurs in a variety of ways. Some examples are:

Changing goals, such as to have another baby, to learn a new skill, to increase one's pledge to the church's budget.

Changing organization structures, such as adding or merging departments, forming new work groups or task forces, or starting a new Sunday School class.

Changing roles, such as employed mothers and home-making fathers, women ministers and male nurses.

Changing processes and procedures, such as using a copier rather than making carbon copies, using a cake mix rather than starting from scratch, or using a guitar as an instrument in Sunday morning worship.

Changing rules or laws, such as the outlawing of segregation or legitimization of gambling.

Changing relationships with others, such as the new employee, the new family at church, the former neighbor.

What happens to us in our relationships with others helps or hurts us. In these relationships, we are changed in constructive and destructive ways.

The smaller worlds we live in are parts of still larger worlds of change—national, international, global. Major events and trends in the world at large challenge our past, call us to an unknown future, and make living in the present complex. Here are but a few of the current trends which impact us, introducing vast amounts of change into our lives to be resisted or accepted:

Shortage of energy sources,

Economic instability,

Religious and political conservatism,

Changing role of women,

Information explosion,

Greater number of retirement-aged people in the population,

Increases in terrorism and crime,

New technologies, and

Rising health care costs.

These trends in our larger world crowd us with life-and-death issues, each of which has the possibility of changing the quality of our lives for better or for worse. We may take these issues seriously and work for positive outcomes. We may discount their importance to us. We may be so overwhelmed by them that we retreat to our smaller, private worlds of experience. We may try to be comfortable with the certainties of our past rather than take on the uncertainties of our future.[2]

The fact of life remains: To live is to change. We can participate in shaping change or we will be shaped by it.

Rate of Change

Change is not a new demand on the human race. What is different in this era of history is the rate of change. We are both privileged and burdened to live in a world that is undergoing major upheavals of change so sweeping they are difficult to comprehend and assimilate. The world-famous physicist, Robert Oppenheimer, said, "This world of ours is a new world. . . . One thing that is new is the prevalence of newness, the changing scale and scope of change itself, so that the world alters as we walk on it, so that the years of a man's life measure not some small growth or rearrangement or modification of what we learned in childhood, but a great upheaval."[3]

Never in history has our world undergone such far-reaching, all-embracing change. In past eras, change came more slowly. For centuries the animal-drawn vehicle transported people. Now in just a few decades, we have moved from automobiles to planes to spaceships. Now the impact of change hits so often and so hard that we find it difficult to adjust. Someone suggested that the slogan for the times we live in should be, "Subject to change without notice."

The increasing rate of change has both affirmed our capacity for changing and left us with tough questions about how much and what kind of change is desirable. What kinds of change will enrich and strengthen us rather than weaken and destroy us?

Change by Any Other Name

My seatmate on a plane recently was returning home from a conference on "How to Be a Change Agent." I asked her how the person doing the training had dealt with the subject.

She said, "The first thing he did was get rid of the word *change*."

I asked, "What did he substitute for it?"

She reported, "He used the terms *growth* and *development*."

We find it easier to deal with change when we state it in positive terms. *Growth* and *development* suggest constructive change. But change does not always bring growth and development. Change can mean people and situations are altered in negative ways. This is one of the reasons I am using the word *change* rather than some other words. Using this word will keep you and me struggling with the negative and positive possibilities in change. We cannot afford to drift into the easy assumption that changes are automatically positive. We need to be able to say no as well as yes to change.

The word *change* is a neutral word. It has no built-in value system. Change is neither intrinsically good nor bad. But what the word implies to us is another matter, for each of us responds to the word differently.

You and I may view change as an exciting, exhilarating possibility. Or, we may view change with suspicion, fear, and dread. The word may even call up images of a crusader or a revolutionary and trigger distorted impressions whether they were intended or not. To some of us, for example, a change in relationship with blacks means interracial marriage, a change in church curriculum means a more liberal theology, a change in moral code means sexual promiscuity, a change in hair style means disrespect for the past, a change in attitude toward war means lack of patriotism. To others, these changes could imply meanings completely opposite to these.

Change by any other name appears easier to deal with. There are many words in our vocabulary which suggest change. A few of these are: *education, training, orientation, supervision, counseling, consulting,* and *parenting*. These terms imply that change will happen, and they carry essentially positive connotations. Because of the positive connotations of these words, these processes are seen as necessary and helpful.

Education suggests positive changes in the knowledge, beliefs, attitudes, values, and behaviors of learners.

Training suggests positive changes in the understandings and skills of trainees.

Orientation suggests positive changes in the amount of information about a new situation on the part of a new person.

Counseling suggests positive changes in the personal functioning of the counselee.

Supervision suggests positive changes in the effectiveness of an employee based on competent and supportive guidance and feedback.

Consultation suggests positive changes in the effectiveness of a client based on the availability of new information and options.

Parenting suggests positive support and guidance for children as they grow and change.

These positive possibilities of change help us open ourselves to education, parenting, training, orientation, counseling, supervision, and other processes. A belief in the possibility of positive results from these processes is what gives us the incentive to be involved in them. But the fact remains that change, even in these positive references, is not always positive.

Change remains what it is: a stark, even harsh and cold word. Change promises no respect for values. Change may help *or* hurt; it may hurt *and* help. Change may destroy *or* develop; it may destroy *and* develop.

No Loose Change

Because change can have negative or positive consequences in our lives, we cannot afford for it to be loose. The changes in our lives need to be linked to a purpose which makes life worth living.

Several years ago a book was written about the results of change in the lives of three women. Titled *Loose Change*, the book described the random ways these women changed in the course of living their lives. Bumped one direction and then another by forces beyond their control, they ended up with life experiences which mirrored their times and environment. Because their lives lacked plan or purpose, they drifted into change. They became victims rather than beneficiaries of change.

Change need not be loose. Even when changes are beyond our control, we are still in control of the responses we make to life's changed conditions. Sometimes we initiate change. Sometimes we respond to change. Either way, the process is similar, although the way we feel about it may be very different.

The Process of Change

Every time we experience change, we go through processes which have some common elements. Some natural forces work in us. Some natural dynamics happen. We may not be aware of these natural elements in change, or we may not understand them, but they happen nevertheless. In fact, as we lift them into full view to look at them, we may feel uncomfortable. Most of us find it much easier to be interested in the results of change than in what happens in the process of changing. But both are important.

It may be time to restate the purpose of the book: To explore what happens to us as we say no and yes to change. The only way to do this is to go behind the scenes, to look below the surface to find out what "makes change tick." Are you ready to continue with me as an explorer?

The quickest way I have found to look at change processes is to state them in a formula. The symbols of a formula allow us to bring several elements into relationship. And, while the formula we use will have some serious inadequacies, it will help introduce a big part of the processes which will be explored in more detail in the rest of the book. The formula may look complicated to you, as any formula always does to me, but it will become more and more clear as we move along.

Here is the formula:

$$A + B + C > D = CHANGE*$$

To understand the formula, you and I have to know what the symbols stand for. Here is the key to unlock that mystery:

A represents a significant level of dissatisfaction with some condition which presently exists.

B represents an awareness of an alternative better condition than what exists.

C represents a knowledge of the first step(s) to take in changing to the better condition.

+ is a plus sign; A and B and C must be added together.

> is a sign which means "greater than." When A, B, and C are added together, the sum of them needs to be greater than D for change to happen.

D represents the costs of making the change.

Change means a new condition brought about by adding to, subtracting from, or replacing an existing condition.

The following paragraphs interpret the formula.

Change occurs when there is a significant level of dissatisfaction with a present condition in my life (A), plus an awareness of an alternative better condition (B), plus a knowledge of the first step(s) to take in changing to the better condition (C): A + B + C. If only dissatisfaction with a present condition is present, change is not likely to happen. If awareness of an alternative better condition is present but there is little dissatisfaction with the current one, change is not likely to happen. Even if a knowledge of a first step to take in changing is present, taking that step is unlikely unless there is enough dissatisfaction with a present condition to commit to changing to a better one.

The sum of A, B, and C must also be greater than the costs of making the change (D). Costs are the time, money, and physical and emotional energy which must be spent in making a change.

Here is an example of how the formula works. Let's assume my change goal is to rebuild my house which was damaged by a tornado (change). The roof on one corner is missing, and two walls on that corner are heavily damaged.

Obviously, I am dissatisfied with the present condition—a damaged house (A). I also am aware of a better condition—the house as it was before the devastating storm. But I also have become aware that in repairing the damaged corner of the house, I could add two needed rooms to the existing structure. So my awareness of a better condition goes beyond merely restoring the old one (B). I also know a first step to take—get an estimate of how much adding the rooms and repairing the other damage will cost and how much insurance money I will have to work with (C).

My dissatisfaction (A), plus my awareness of a better condition (B), plus my knowledge of the first step (C) bring me to a point where I can begin to weigh costs.

I may decide the longer amount of time it will take to build as well as repair the house is worth it. I may decide that the additional cost beyond the insurance adjustment is an amount I can afford (D). In this case, I move ahead with the change. New information might modify the change goal, but the change process will begin to happen.

This illustration is relatively simple. Change processes, as you and I both know, are much more complex. There are many dynamic forces at work. What about all the other forces influencing my change goal? I decided to rebuild the existing house, but there must have been several options I considered and rejected, such as moving to a completely different house. What about all the other things which must be considered in making a decision about what to do? What about the sense of loss I felt about the old condition of the house which will never be the same again? In making the changes, how am I going to manage the differences between my opinions and those of other family members and between me and the builders about the specifics of the building project? Conflict could happen. These kinds of things are essential considerations in change processes too.

A house is a thing, an *it*. As essential and important as material possessions we own and use are, they in no way compare to changes in us as persons. Change happens to us in very, very personal ways shaping and reshaping how we see ourselves, how others see us, and how God sees us. The change formula generally works in these areas, too, but the dynamics of change are much more complex.

Renewing Change

Since change can help or hurt, and since the process of changing is complex—even mysterious, we need to choose deliberately the changes which will renew and strengthen us. We need skills in change processes which will facilitate positive growth in ourselves and in others.

Constructive change brings us an inner awareness of ourselves so that we better understand our own feelings, wants, needs, and longings. Constructive change brings us outward awareness so we relate more responsively and responsibly to others and to the world God created for us. Constructive change brings us into stronger, more responsive connection with the source of all life and growth—God.

God is the great change agent. He offers us purpose in life which is so stable and enduring it has stood the test of time. His enduring purpose for our world, for our shared life, and for us as individuals gives us a firm foundation for constructing our changing goals, activities, and relationships. God invites us to the new: new faith, new hope, and new love. New life. He reveals his plans for us, and his plan is so good it creates dissatisfaction in us with life which misses the mark of his intentions. He holds out to us the better conditions of life lived in his Spirit and the ultimate gift of eternal life. Change. God offers us the possibility of renewing change—change which regenerates us and restores us to a right relationship with him, with each other, and with our universe. "The whole creation is on tiptoe to see the wonderful sight of the sons of God coming into their own" (Rom. 8:19, Phillips).

The process of renewing change is unending in God's design of us and our world. Birth and death. Ages and stages. Seasons. Salvation. Reconciliation. And more. In Christ we learn the qualities which help us change in ways which renew and strengthen us.

Christ expressed an openness toward life and toward people. He was open toward people even when they were strange and different from him. In the presence of Christ, persons of many backgrounds found the freedom to be themselves. He was open toward them. He put people in no rigid categories, although he was aware of the categories in his day.

Jesus' life was also characterized by expectancy. He accepted persons as they were and saw in them the possibility of change. He issued imperatives believing persons could act on them: "Give to him that asketh." "Come, . . . follow me." "Seek, and ye shall find." Not only persons but also times change. Jesus anticipated a new age, a new order. He was never overcome by the status quo (what is)—although it killed him.

Jesus' life expressed the quality of creativity. Jesus not only expected change but also produced it. He taught, and people listened. He was faithful, and they acquired faith. He suffered, and in his suffering his followers were renewed—redeemed.

What better qualities for renewing change than openness, expectancy, and creativity. These things we do by seeking renewing change in faith—faith which looks to Jesus as model and to God for present strength, which God's Spirit gives.

I remember being deeply moved while reading the play *A Child Is Born* by Stephen Vincent Benet. The setting was in the inn in Bethlehem where Christ was born in a stable out back. The inn was crowded with people of money, seekers of pleasure. The innkeeper's wife was portrayed as a sad, somewhat bitter person struggling with grief over the death of a child. The inn crowd was unaware of the birth of the Child in the stable, but the innkeeper's wife knew about it. An awareness of the significance of the event began to settle over her. Meaning awakened in her. In a moment of boldness, she addressed the crowd in the inn. Her speech was poignant indictment of herself and ourselves for our blindness to the blessed vision of hope and the brightness of change. Shackled by our hurt, bitterness, uncaring ways, and compromised time, we cannot move to follow the vision. Not even if we dare look upon it.

In the play, the innkeeper's wife reminds us that we can lose the essence of life among the rubble of misplaced loves. She calls the crowd to rise up from their mediocrity and to grasp the vision of the miracle among them. She knew full well the night had produced an event destined to change the world. And with it the people in Bethlehem had to change.

And so it is, then and now. In Bethlehem and unto the uttermost parts of the earth. Life is lost less by dying, than by denying the dream.

For Your Reflection

1. Make a list of some of the bigger changes you have experienced during the past year. (The following categories might help you recall the changes: living conditions, health, relationships, possessions, ideas, attitudes, skills, time used.) Which changes did you choose, and

which were forced on you? Which changes are pluses and which ones are minuses in your life? To what extent were you aware of the process you went through in each of these changes?

2. Identify three changes you would like to see happen in your life in the next year. Use the formula explained on pages 26-27 in thinking about making these changes.

3

God, invade this new day with courage;
Place in my hands both
   the stability of past securities
and the pull of possibilities.
God, steady me
   while I risk something new.

—Billie Pate

3

Keeping Our Balance

He saw me arrive as he nonchalantly tossed a basket-ball into the backyard goal. His eyes flashed a welcome, and a boyish grin spread across his face. I felt his tight, warm hug as his feet left the ground in his reach for my neck.

When I stepped back to see my nephew, Jeff, whom I had not seen for several months, I saw a too-small T-shirt stretched across his expanding chest and a buttonhole at the waist of his jeans which was barely passing the "stress test." He had changed! The little boy was growing up.

In an instant I felt an incredible mix of emotions— happiness about his growing up, sadness that the "little boy" would soon be gone forever, giving way to the turbu-lent developmental stage called adolescence. *No teenager can ever love an aunt like a little boy*, I thought. *I liked him just the way he was.*

Briefly I resisted seeing Jeff change. Then I was able to feel joy about his growing up, accepting the fact that our relationship will change in the process, but hoping and risking that it can change for the better.

When was the last time you felt a little tug-of-war going on inside you? Wanting change *versus* not wanting change.

Two opposing kinds of forces bombard us constantly —forces *for* change and forces *against* change. Both are natural because we not only need change but we also need stability. A good balance in life includes both. The chang-

---

ing parts of life need to be balanced by the unchanging parts. Once we understand what seems to be a contradiction, we can move more smoothly in the flow of change, balancing life by sometimes accepting change and by sometimes resisting it.

Dynamic Equilibrium

The delicate balance we maintain between change and stability is called equilibrium. Equilibrium is not static; it is dynamic. We establish equilibrium, and we keep reestablishing it. In trying to maintain the balance of our lives, this question is often with us: "How can we live at the interface between the constant and the dependable, which we must have as a base line of life, and the surprising, the flexible, the adaptive, and the emerging which we need to make life live?"[1] The answer: By balancing stability and change in our lives. By establishing and restoring equilibrium.

Maintaining equilibrium is a common experience in the physical sense. Walking a railroad track, standing on a fence, and riding a bicycle are examples of situations that require balancing physical forces which pull from different directions. In these situations, we balance the various forces operating within and upon us. By subtle shifts in position, we balance our total response. We maintain equilibrium; we establish balance.

Just as equilibrium operates in the physical realm, it also operates in the psychological, social, and spiritual realms. Conditions of change and no-change exist side by side. And, while periods of change may be different from periods of relative stability, the two states contain the same set of opposing and interacting forces. Equilibrium is the temporary balance we achieve in the midst of these competing forces.

To resist or to change.

To stay in place or to move.

To reject new evidence or to accept it.

SAY NO, SAY YES TO CHANGE

To rely on well-developed skills or to develop and adapt to new ones.

To maintain an attitude or to modify it.

Opposing forces sustain the equilibrium of our lives—driving forces (change) and restraining forces (resistance). Between these two sets of forces, dynamic equilibrium is established and maintained.[2]

Any factor that increases willingness to change can be called a force toward change, a *change force*. Any factor that decreases willingness to change can be called a force against change, a *resistance force*.[3]

A father may be dissatisfied with the amount of time he spends with his family. His love for his family is a driving force, causing him to desire to increase (change) the amount of time he spends with his family. On the other hand, his commitment to his job competes with increasing his time commitment to his family (resistance). Somewhere between the two sets of forces the father establishes equilibrium. This equilibrium may be disturbed and reestablished at higher or lower levels as the father continues to deal with balancing his time with his family with his time at work.

Remember the formula in chapter 2—A + B + C > D=change. Resistance to change comes from being satisfied with conditions as they exist, from a lack of vision of any alternative better conditions, from fearing or not knowing the first step toward change, from insecurity about what may be required in future steps, from an unwillingness to pay the cost to make a change. Change forces, by contrast, come from dissatisfaction, from a vision of a better alternative, from a sense of security about taking the first step, and from the belief that the change will be worth the cost.

Change always disturbs the steady state we have established—our equilibrium—by requiring us to consider something new. Resistance causes us to defend the equilibrium we have established against change.

Equilibrium as Status Quo

Equilibrium seems like a vague concept, but it does exist in identifiable forms. Equilibrium is status quo—the *what is* of life, the existing condition of our lives at a given point in time. Equilibrium is never completely permanent, although *what is* can be relatively stable. Status quo changes from moment to moment, day-to-day, year-to-year. It is expressed in many forms, such as:

Beliefs—facts and intuitive data we hold to be true, such as "Columbus discovered America in 1492," "Jack is a liberal," or "eagles fly."

Attitudes—beliefs we focus on a specific object and feel emotion about, such as patriotism toward country or prejudice toward people of another race or creed.

Values—core beliefs of ultimate importance to us, such as freedom, faith, love.

Habits—patterned behavior which is automatic and involuntary, such as always buying the same brand, going to church every Sunday, interrupting other people as they speak.

Relationships—bonds of dependence and interdependence with other people, such as husband and wife, parents and children, members of a Sunday School class, partners in a business venture, friends.

Roles—expected behavior within specific functions or positions, such as president, mother, chairperson, manager, counselor.

Social structures—ways we relate to each other in accomplishing specific purposes, such as family, club, church, work group.

Social norms—behavior expected from us by groups to which we belong which is enforced through acceptance or nonacceptance in the group, such as being rational rather than emotional in a work setting, wearing a certain type of clothes to a wedding, or accepting only a man or only a woman in a particular role.

Policies, rules, laws—behaviors required from us by

SAY NO, SAY YES TO CHANGE

groups to which we belong which are punishable if violated, such as speed limits, zoning restrictions, lunch and break schedules at work.

Schedules—frequency, length, and time of routine activities, such as meeting and meal times and deadlines for filing tax returns.

Life is patterned in predictable ways. These patterns help us deal with the demands on us. Much of this patterning has the labels of the above list—beliefs, attitudes, values, habits, relationships, roles, structures, norms, rules, and schedules. These control our thought processes and behavior. They are acquired bit-by-bit and piece-by-piece; they are reinforced through use. They enable us to act without thinking about every step. Given a set of circumstances, we know how to respond in preprogramed ways.

Take habit, for example. Teethbrushing is a habit for most of us. We do not consciously think: *First, I'll pick up the toothbrush and toothpaste; then I will put the toothbrush under running water to get it wet, then I will put paste on the brush*, and so forth. The sequence of behavior is automatic. When you and I first learned to brush our teeth, we had to think about every step, but that is no longer necessary. Habit is established.

Life would be burdensome without habits. If we had to think through every action we take, if there were no routines to depend on, life would require even more expenditure of energy than it does. Through habit we put in place behaviors we can call on as needed—patterns for eating, sleeping, making a phone call.

Habits are dependable and relatively stable. They automatically function for us with a minimum investment of energy (unless they are neurotic habits which take a lot of energy to keep operating). Through habit our limited physical and emotional energies are conserved to invest in novel experiences.

Just as some habits serve us personally, certain patterns serve us in relationships with others. In the work setting, we pattern our relationships in getting work done into organization structure, goals, positions, and roles. How we are expected to function within an organization and in a role is further spelled out through such things as norms, policies, and procedures. We are highly conscious of all these understandings as they are being developed or as we are learning them. But, once in place, these patterns and routines begin to trigger automatic behaviors. They conserve what has come to have meaning and value to us. They become relatively stable.

While such things as habits, norms, and laws have very valuable functions, they also can enslave us. There is no slavery which can compare to the ingrained habits of sin which get imbedded in us or incorporated into the norms, laws, and rules of our collective life.

A passage in Isaiah paints the picture: "The wicked are like the tossing of the sea; for it cannot rest, and its waters toss up mire and dirt" (Isa. 57:20, RSV). The sea produces mire because of its natural water motions. The same can be true of us. When sin is imbedded in the structures of our lives and of our society, the natural motions of our lives (habits, norms, etc.) produce the mire and dirt of sin.

The opposite also is true. When goodness and righteousness are imbedded in the patterns of our lives, the natural motions of life produce good.

Stability

To deal with life, we need stability and continuity. The habits, norms, rules, etc. we develop to create stability in our lives become comfortable. If they are effective, they require little effort to maintain. Even when they are inherently bad, they are dependable. Even when they don't work at all, they are a known quantity with which to deal. They become highly resistant to change.

This helps explain why many people stay locked into undesirable relationships and limiting circumstances throughout life. Dealing with the "knowns" of a miserable existence appears easier than dealing with the "unknowns" of trying to change the situation. Problems in the status quo—what is—are preferable to the risks of something new.

A woman silently endures a relationship with a mate who severely abuses her physically because there is security in knowing the mate is a source of support for her and the children. The unknowns about rebuilding this security on another base are too great to risk change.

A church gets comfortable with its routine ways of doing things, repeating the same cycle of activities year after year. Members live off the past—the known—without dealing realistically with new information about their emerging future—the unknown.

An employer cultivates employees to tell him only what he wants to hear. His inability to receive feedback undermines the effectiveness of his position because he does not receive the information he needs to make corrections in his operation—change.

When the status quo of our lives works well for us and for others, we are blessed, indeed. But, more important, when the status quo of our lives is based on Christian beliefs and values, *what is* is something to be defended and preserved. Unnecessary change can be resisted with confidence. But when the status quo of our lives is out of touch with Christian values, is hurtful to us or to others, we need an openness to change—the redeeming work of God in our lives.

The longer each of us lives and the longer we stay in the same groups, the more our habits and routines become hardened by time and tradition. We are less upset by minor stresses, tensions, and crises. On the other hand, younger persons and newer groups are affected by the slightest disturbance. As you have noticed, young children change very rapidly in response to influences upon them while change tends to be more difficult for older persons.

The older person has had years to establish routines. The group which has been in existence for years, as a family or club, has had time to build traditions and norms. Time has a way of overtaking the raw spontaneity, flexibility, and adaptability of a new person or group and regimenting life into stable patterns of functioning. Great capacities for maintaining equilibrium are established. Younger persons and newer groups, by contrast, are much more vulnerable to change forces.

Jesus understood the dynamics of stability and change in our lives. He sat a child in the midst of the people he was teaching and said, "Unless you . . . become as little children, you will never get into the Kingdom" (Matt. 18:3, TLB).

A young child is impressionable, open, spontaneous, adaptable, trusting, and risking. A young child changes easily. Children have not yet experienced the stubborn stability of adulthood which is less impressionable, less open, less spontaneous and adaptable, less trusting and risking. The adult tendency is toward stability because so much of the growing and building of life is completed. The child's tendency is toward change because so many of the growing and building tasks of life are still ahead. The truly mature person—regardless of age—integrates the capacity both for stability and for change.

Paul wrote to the church at Ephesus about being mature followers of Christ—full grown in the Lord. He reminded them that while entry to the kingdom requires the childlike quality of being able to change, mature discipleship requires *change* and *stability* based on truth in Christ.

We will no longer be like children, forever changing our minds about what we believe because someone has told us something different, or has cleverly lied to us and made the lie sound like truth. Instead, we will lovingly follow the truth at all times— speaking truly, dealing truly, living truly—and so become more and more in every way like Christ (Eph. 4:14-15, TLB).

Change Forces

Change in our lives comes from two sources—from our pain and from our possibilities. Situations of threat and crises which bring us pain are fertile soil in which change forces grow. But change also develops out of unclaimed possibilities in our lives—the difference between what is and what could be, between belief and action, between theory and practice. Pain caused by crisis and not-yet-realized possibility creates situations of dissatisfaction which become powerful motivators to change.

In crises situations, a person or group hurts because of loss or unsolved problems. Old routines are no longer adequate to cope with newer circumstances.

A church in an inner city, for example, experiences a steady decline in membership. A majority of the church members have moved to the suburbs and commute to church. There is a gap between the educational, social, and economic backgrounds of church members and people living in the church neighborhood. Neighborhood people need the ministry of the church, but the church lacks both the sensitivity to the need and the resources to minister in the community. Crisis is felt because the traditional programs of the church are not as effective as they once were. Even when the church conducts its same programs well, the usual good results do not happen. Membership declines. Giving drops.

A child with a physical impairment is born into a family. The entire family experiences crisis in learning to respond to the special needs of the child.

A person loses a job and has to face the panic and crisis of no income in the face of everyday expenses which do not cease.

Change forces come not just from crises however. The urge to change also arises out of our natural tendencies to grow and develop, to become more of what God created you and me to be.

A Sunday School teacher attends a conference in which she learns about ways to improve Bible teaching in a Sunday School class. She senses what the new ideas could mean to her class. She shares the information with her fellow teachers. Together they find ways to improve Bible teaching in their own church. New possibilities are claimed!

In a training session I once conducted, I asked participants to list three changes they would like to have happen in their family settings. Some of the changes the persons desired were:

More time together as a family;
Better communication with a teenager;
Less TV viewing by children;
A new house;
Added skill in providing sex education for children;
More family worship and sharing.

I requested each participant to reflect on the list just made. I then asked, "Is your desire for change growing out of your pain or out of possibilities not yet claimed in your life?" Some gave quick and clearcut answers.

After more thought, however, one person said, "I thought my interest in change was caused by pain: but, the more I thought of it, I realized my pain was pushing me toward new possibilities."

Another commented, "We are trying to claim a new possibility, but trying to do that is painful."

Loss, alienation, grief, hurt, and disappointment may look like unlikely places to encounter change until we remember that the experiences of life which break up our comfortable routines also open up new possibilities.

This has been true in my own life time after time. At one time I was in a job that reached a dead end; then, suddenly, I discovered a whole new world of opportunity I could never have seen if I hadn't needed to see it. On another occasion, an illness put me to bed for a couple of weeks. During these moments of interruption in the routines of my life, I got many new insights for living. Change in the midst of crisis.

One oriental culture has a symbol for crisis which can be translated "opportunity." And this may be the idea a poet was expressing:

The deeper that sorrow carves into your being,
the more joy you can contain.
Is not the cup that holds your wine the very cup
that was burned at the potter's oven?
And is not the lute that soothes your spirit,
the very wood that was hollowed with knives?[4]

Followers of Christ see this clearly in the death and resurrection of Jesus. After the deep hurt, disappointment, and despair of the crucifixion came the bright, new, triumphant hope of the resurrection.

Once a change begins to happen, there is a natural tendency for one change to create need for additional changes—a domino effect. One part of our lives touched with change can set in motion a chain reaction because one aspect of life is always intertwined with others.

A child develops from childhood into adolescence and relationships between child and parent must change.

The last child leaves home creating an "empty nest" for parents who are faced with adjusting their relationship with each other.

A new pastor leads a congregation. Eventually his commitment and leadership style impact the church, bringing about change in the congregation.

A spouse who is an alcoholic stops drinking and the whole family has to reorient its life to sobriety rather than drunkenness.

Tax laws are changed, causing accounting systems to change and causing a need for new skills by persons handling the new system.

Resistance Forces

Anything which reduces willingness to make a change may be a resistance force. Resistance may be rational or irrational, recognized or unrecognized, general or specific. Resistance may occur early or late in a change process. Resistance forces are usually expressed in general opposition to change, inability to change, and desire to preserve the status quo—all variations on the same theme.

"I am tired of our church using popular music forms in congregational worship" (a general opposition to change).

"We have always met on Tuesday; I can't adjust my schedule to meet on another day" (an inability to change).

"I don't see any need to purchase a new car. I like the car we have!" (a desire to preserve the status quo).

Resistance forces often emerge while we are in the midst of changing. Sometimes we feel resistance to how a change is being handled. Sometimes we experience resistance because we are not in enough agreement with a change to see it through. Sometimes we are called on to change too fast, and we have to resist enough to slow down the change process. Sometimes the satisfaction we derived from changing is so low that we resist further change.

Interference Forces

Interference forces are ones which interfere with change but which are not directly related to the change itself.[5] Interference forces are not opposed to change; they divert energy away from change.

Interference forces usually arise around resources of time, energy, and money. Sometimes there are insufficient resources to accomplish a particular change—not enough money to take a trip, not enough time to enroll in a night course. At other times almost all available resources are being used to maintain a current situation, leaving few resources available for significant change.

When a family member is severely ill, the illness makes such heavy demands on the family's money, time, and energy that no new family projects can be undertaken during the illness. Family time is spent on maintenance. The illness interferes with most new experiences the family might otherwise choose.

Some churches, for example, are incapable of significant change because of interference forces. The resources

SAY NO, SAY YES TO CHANGE

of the church are used up in merely surviving. Interest in changing may be strong but resources are too limited to undertake or sustain new, more effective ministries. Such a church is having to expend more money and energy than it is taking in. Surviving as a church is an issue to be dealt with before the cost of additional change can be absorbed.

The pastor comments to a deacon, "Every time I bring up the matter of starting a day-care center to minister to working mothers in the community, the idea is opposed. Why?"

The deacon replies, "I don't sense that we are opposing the idea. Most of our members feel this ministry is needed, but where do we get the money to do it?"

"Do you think funding the project is the *issue*?"

"Yes," says the deacon.

If we are unaware of interference forces, we may interpret some forces which work against change as resistance when they are not. Sometimes interference, not resistance, is at work in our lives.

Analyzing Forces in Change

The reason for knowing about types of forces and how to recognize them is so we can make them work for us and not against us. Change and stability come about through proper management of both the yes and no forces. Recognizing forces which work for and against change, or which interfere with change, puts us in a better position to work with them.

A technique to help us identify and deal with forces for and against change is sometimes referred to as a "for/against list" or a "pro/con list."[6] The technique works this way: We list on a sheet of paper the forces we identify as working for change in one column and the forces working against change in another column.

An affluent family I read about decided to change to a more simple life-style. The family decided to spend only one-half of its income on itself and to give one-half of its income to help alleviate world hunger. Here are only a few of the forces they identified which worked for and against this change:

For	Against
Biblical teachings which support caring for the hungry	Friends and work associates who consider this behavior strange, not normative.
Joy in sharing scarce resources with others.	Insecurity about what the future might hold if too much money is shared and not enough is laid away for future use.
Reduced complexity because of less money to spend: fewer buying decisions, more reliance on natural resources, more no-cost entertainment, and more personally made gifts.	Peer pressure on kids at school because they are different; parents unsure to what extent the choice is internalized by their children as well as by them.

In understanding the forces which work for and against change, we develop a healthy respect for restraining as well as driving forces in change. A considerable amount of stability is needed to absorb change. Stability builds the sense of security we need to deal with the risk-taking of change.

Change comes about, then, as we alter the balance between change and resistance forces. There are at least three ways in which this balance can be altered in bringing about change: (1) eliminating a force or reducing the intensity of a force, such as dealing enough with the reasons for saying yes or no so that a particular reason is no longer as valid or important as it once was; (2) adding to or strengthening forces, such as by furnishing new information to support a yes or no; (3) changing the direction of forces, such as turning a no force into a yes force. The most effective ways to reduce, increase, or change the direction of forces are through more information, through more experience, through more assurances from trusted persons, and through participation in decision making as change is made.

An illustration of analyzing change forces and working with them creatively is the following example I observed as an elementary school principal led faculty members to consider changing the curriculum resources being used in their school. The principal analyzed the major forces working for and against change as follows:

For	Against
The new curriculum plan is supported by a group of parents.	The curriculum resources are more costly than the ones now being used.
The superintendent of schools supports the new curriculum plan.	Teachers are afraid they will not be skilled enough to use the new resources.
Two teachers out of eight have taught in other schools where the proposed curriculum resources were used, and they like them; they say the curriculum plan provides a lot of room for teacher creativity.	Use of the new curriculum resources will require some retraining of teachers to use them.
The curriculum plan is more experience oriented and will appeal to the interest and needs of class members.	Some teachers feel the curriculum does not have a strong enough content orientation.

In working with change, the principal took the following action:

The principal explained that the costs of changing to the new curriculum were not prohibitive and could be cared for within budget limitations. Assurances which could be given were given. Once this was done, a force may have been eliminated as an interference force. Or, if cost was a superficial resistance force, the true resistance might shift to another point.

The principal circulated sample copies of curriculum resources to teachers so they could judge them for themselves. The amount of available information was increased. This action could remove or reduce a resistance force or make a change force out of a resistance force if materials are satisfactory to teachers reviewing them. The information also could turn a change force into a resistance force if the resources were unsatisfactory to the teachers—a risk the principal took.

The principal requested teachers who had previously used the curriculum resources successfully to have an open discussion with other teachers about the advantages of the curriculum plan. A change force was strengthened by sharing positive, personal experience.

The principal met with teachers who had never used the resources to determine what training would be necessary, if any, for them to feel equipped to use the new curriculum plan. A plan for a training session was an outgrowth of this meeting. A force for change was strengthened. A resistance force shifted to become a change force through allowing participation in decision making.

A careful analysis of any situation gives clues to how to work with change. Many of us are more sensitive to change forces. We recognize them within ourselves but tend to see resistance forces operating predominately in others. As this happens, we get into the habit of seeing resistance as something always to be overcome. We need to work, then, at accurately identifying and stating both sets of forces. After clarifying them, we can work at modifying both change and resistance forces based on more information, more experience, more support and assurance, more involvement of persons in decisions affecting them.

Through reorienting ourselves to the yes and no forces in change, we can give attention to both the driving forces and the restraining forces in life. We can say no with more assurance when we need to. We can say yes with more confidence when it is the right answer.

Discovery of constructive change forces opens the possibility of adding to or strengthening these forces. When you and I are trying to help positive change happen, we have the option of joining and strengthening the natural flow of change, as the school principal did, rather than feeling we must start by overpowering resistance. When it is possible, freeing natural change forces is much more pleasant work than overcoming resistance.

Life is a balancing act between forces for and against change. We can expect to say no and yes to change all of our lives. We initiate change. We control a lot of the change in our lives. Even when we lost our capacity to say *no*, we can still control how we will respond to the changes which come our way. We are more "in control" of change when we understand how to work with our natural tendencies to change and to resist change because it takes both stability and change to maintain the balance of our lives.

For Your Reflection

1. Identify a relatively small, but important change you would like to see happen in your life. Write it down. In two columns list all the reasons you can think of for and against making the change.

2. Identify a fairly major change you long to see happen in your life. Write it down. Then do the following:

(1)   List the forces working for and against the change.

(2)   Study each force for and against change, asking yourself these questions:

   • Is the force a change force, a resistance force, or an interference force?

   • Is there a way I can eliminate or reduce this force for or against change? How? When?

   • Is there a way I can add to or strengthen this force? How? When?

   • Is there a way to transform a force against change into a force for change? Or to transform a force for change into a force against change? How? When?

4

Lord,
Forgive me this day
my failing to sense the miracle of newness
   of minute, and hour, and day
   in every encounter along the way,
the spellbound grandeur of the new.

—Billie Pate

4
Saying Yes
to Change

While visiting the Museum of Natural History in Chicago, I was fascinated by an exhibit commemorating an anniversary of the museum. One part of the exhibit described the process of collecting historical articles to be placed in the museum. A brief excerpt from an interview with museum collectors was reported. The collectors were asked, "At what moment does the collector find his greatest pleasure?"

One collector replied, "The moment of discovery."

Another added, "The moment of acquisition."

For all of us, some of the great moments in life are our moments of discovery and acquisition. Our moments of discovery are the ah-ha moments when an idea comes to life, a meaning becomes clear, or we see a thing of beauty for the very first time. We may discover and enjoy without acquiring, of course, but there are special joys in acquiring something as our very own—whether it is an idea, an object, a skill, a relationship, an attitude, a value, or a new behavior. Ownership is saying yes to something in the very deepest sense. We decide about it. We make it our own! We change.

Levels of Change

Not all change happens at the same level. Some changes are superficial and unstable—here today and gone tomorrow. Other changes are deep and stable—they have an enduring quality.

I like this definition of change: Change is a new condition which is self-maintaining.[1] We could stop the definition after "a new condition," but the phrase "which is self-maintaining" implies something very significant. A change has been acquired and is securely in place. It belongs. It is internalized. The change is owned by someone or by some group. A person or group has genuinely said yes to the change—has made a decision about it and a commitment to it.

Not all change occurs at this deep level however. There are at least three levels at which change occurs: compliance, identification, and internalization.[2] Let's explore these three words and the ideas behind them.

1. *Compliance.* When we change at the compliance level, we are giving in to the request or demands of others for change. We change because we have to. Someone in authority over us makes a decision for us and requires us to change, or an event beyond our control forces change.

A parent demands of a child, "Stop slamming the door." The child stops.

A supervisor tells a perpetually late employee, "Start arriving on time or you will lose your job." The employee changes his arrival patterns.

A church decides to form Sunday School classes based on age and sex of members, and adult church members change classes accordingly.

The Supreme Court rules that segregation in public schools is illegal. Segregation ends and a lot of conduct changes, though some old attitudes hang on.

We do many things differently because we feel required to. If we continue to do them simply because we are required, we are merely complying with authority or circumstance. The "new condition" has limited meaning to us. We do what we must because we have no other option. We do what is required to satisfy someone else. We do what is demanded because we do not want to pay the price for not doing it. We do what is required best when some-

SAY NO, SAY YES TO CHANGE

one in authority is looking over our shoulder. And, while we do what is required, we have a strong tendency to revert to old behaviors—like exceeding the speed limit on the interstate when a highway patrol car is not in sight or complaining about a new decision when the "boss" is not present.

Authority is necessary in life, as is compliance with authority. A parent instructs a child to stop and look both directions before crossing a street. Whether the child fully understands or agrees with the instruction, it is important that the instruction be heeded. Compliance on the part of the child is appropriate. Compliance saves life and limb for the child even if he is doing what he is told to do only to avoid punishment.

Authority structures and authority figures usually intend to work for our best interest. In actuality, they may or may not. But as long as they have legitimate authority over us—whether granted by us or someone else—we must comply or pay the consequences.

When we change because we are required to by an external authority, the enforcer of the condition is unstable. When the authority is not looking or is not present, we tend to revert easily to earlier beliefs, attitudes, and behaviors.

For example, if the Supreme Court decision in 1954 outlawing school segregation were suddenly abolished, it is possible many people who were committed to segregation would revert to earlier patterns of relationships with blacks. For these people, little deep, abiding change has occurred in their thinking and feeling about blacks. Their changed behavior is compliant behavior. Remove the requirements to comply and much of the "old condition" would move back into place.

Another example is the college student who leaves home for the first time, leaving behind the values and standards of his parents for very different standards of conduct in his new setting. His sudden change in behavior in the college setting may indicate the student was merely complying with certain standards under the watchful eye of the parent.

I have known churches, as you probably have, in which great changes occurred under the leadership of a particular pastor; but, once the pastor left, the church changed almost overnight to its old ways. Members of the church may have been only complying with the leadership of the pastor or identifying strongly with him as a leader.

Changing through compliance is necessary and is effective in a limited way. But it is only the minimum level of change. The next highest level is identification.

2. *Identification.* At the identification level, we change more on our own although we are still dependent on others in making the change. In identification, we identify two things: our own wants and needs for change, and attractive models (examples) who exhibit the change in which we are interested. Either may come first—the realization of our wants and need or the recognition of an attractive model. Our wants/needs and our choice of models may be conscious or unconscious. These two connect in almost automatic ways. We may understand what is happening to us at the time, or we may understand it only much later when we review the past.

A boy mirrors his father's behavoir. The father is a role model of an adult male to the son. People comment about the son, "He's a chip off the old block," meaning he is like his father.

Leaders in a church spot other churches doing a superb job of reaching people or ministering to families. They model their church program after what they can observe or learn from other churches.

A person is elected to a position. He studies the leadership pattern of other persons who have occupied the position previously. He tries to mirror the best of their actions.

A married couple become parents. They rely on what they learned from parents who most influenced them.

When I was a teenager, I changed my handwriting style to a backward slant. I could not have explained why at the time, but now I know two things probably converged—my need as an adolescent to establish my own unique identity and the handwriting style of my dad's cousin whom I admired very much. Clara Walker was my model for handwriting. I copied her style until a unique expression of it became my very own. I changed through identification.

Models are essential to us. Models give us preliminary patterns we can copy as they are or which we can adjust to our own unique requirements. One person or a group of persons may be our model. Or, we may choose the best from several models and put together a composite model which influences us. The model does not have to be present. We do not have to know the model personally. We may know about the model through reading, through watching television, in hearing about the person, or in other ways.

Identification is an internal and an external process. We are dependent on others who serve us as models, but we control internally the extent to which we copy or mirror the model. We select. Through identification, we decide to adapt a pattern to fit ourselves. This opens the creative possibility that we can end up not as a poor imitation but as the real thing.

Identification is a higher level of change than compliance. If we copy or mirror someone else, we can keep doing this so long as we have a pattern to go by. But, when we redesign the pattern of the model to fit ourselves and make it our own, we move to the highest level of change—internalization.

3. *Internalization.* When we internalize change—make it our own—we are no longer dependent on external authority or on an attractive model to keep change in our lives in place. The new condition is in place because it has been made a part of you or me. We believe in, feel strongly about, value, and decide to change to the new condition.

We act out of our inner commitment to the change.

A part of my training and experience is in education. The primary goal of education, of course, is bringing about change in learners. I have been a teacher and an administrator in public schools, in church educational programs, and in higher education. The teaching-learning process intrigues and delights me.

As a teacher, I am always an authority figure calling on students to comply with the authority of knowledge, educational structures, and my own guidance of learning process—hopefully in their best interest. A certain amount of compliance is inevitable.

For some students—though not all by any means—I am a model of what is being taught or how it is being taught. I cannot choose to be a model, I can only be available as one. The student chooses. For students who view me as a model, there is a match between who I am and what I know and what the student wants or needs. There is a match between my style of teaching and the student's style of learning. Identification happens.

With a few students, I am able to experience the unspeakable joy of being present as they take my teaching into their private worlds of experience and make it their very own. The content being learned is no longer my content to be given back verbatim on an examination; the content has useful meaning and value for the student—two dimes and a nickle not only add up to a quarter, but knowning this helps get the right change back at the candy counter. Internalization happens.

If I am secure enough as a teacher to let internalization happen, the student in a real sense outgrows a dependent need for me as teacher. The student and I become interdependent. We become fellow pilgrims in the common pursuit of learning. Sometimes the student is my teacher, and I am learner; sometimes I am the teacher, and the student is learner. This does not change our titles of *student* and *teacher*, nor does it change the status or formal authority difference between us in an educational system.

But it does change our relationship. We are learning associates. The student is taking initiative to internalize knowledge beyond the limits of my teaching.

Parents have had similar experiences with their children. I remember a dedicated Christian couple who were thoroughly committed to missions. At first, their children went to regular meetings of church missions organizations for children simply because they were taken (compliance). They gave some of their first allowance money to missions because they saw their parents give (identification). Then, as they grew up, the children internalized a commitment to missions of their very own. One of them made a commitment to give a significant amount of her income to missions. The other child responded to God's call to be a missionary. It all started with compliance—being taken as a small child to a meeting.

I have helped develop curriculum materials for churches. In putting together a Sunday School pupil's quarterly, we work with the concept of learning tasks. The most general statement of task for every learner in the Christian education process is: listening with growing alertness to the gospel and responding in faith and love.[3] This task has meaning for learners of all ages and for any one learner throughout his lifetime. There are four more specific learning tasks which we try to build into pupil materials. They illustrate the internalization process.

(1) Exploring all of life's relationships in light of the gospel (the Bible deals with a person's relationship to other people, to God, to history, and to all of God's creative uiverse).

(2) Discovering Christian meaning and value in life's relationships.

(3) Appropriating Christian meaning and value personally.

(4) Assuming personal and social responsibility in light of the Christian gospel.[4]

Explore. Discover. Appropriate meaning and value. Assume personal and social responsibility. As we move into deeper levels of learning, we are more likely to internalize meaning and value from what we learn. Meaning and value, once internalized, form the basis for responsible action in life.

Internalization is the ideal in Christian education just as internalization is the objective of all education. Enduring changes in behavior are the real proof that learning has taken place. The most convincing behavior is the natural, unaffected behavior which comes from a match between what a person professes to believe and value and who he is in attitude and behavior. "Be doers of the word, and not hearers only" (Jas. 1:22, RSV).

Changing in Relationship to God

In working with the concepts of compliance, identification, and internalization, it has occurred to me that God makes himself known to us in such a way that we can learn of him at all three of these levels. He relates to us in ways which make it possible for us to say yes to him at the deepest level. God works with us as an authority person (Father), as a model (Son), and as an internalized living presence within us (Holy Spirit).

God the Father is a God of authority. He is a God of concern, justice, and wrath—jealous of our own best interests. God the Father calls on us to comply with his authority and to accept the consequences of noncompliance. The Ten Commandments are an expression of God's authority.

God, as Son, expresses himself in human as well as divine terms. "The Word became flesh and dwelt among us" (John 1:14, RSV). Jesus is Redeemer, but he also is a model with whom we can identify, one we can emulate and copy. He is a standard against which we can test ourselves. Jesus is God incarnate in human form, "a man of sorrows, and acquainted with grief" (Isa. 53:3). Jesus is the Way, the Truth, and the Life in terms humankind can comprehend and with whom humankind can identify.

Just as "Jesus was the revelation of God in history; the Spirit is the realization of God in experience. Jesus was the incarnation of God in a human life; the Spirit is the reincarnation of God in Christians."[5] God, as Spirit, is our present help—our mentor. To the Christian, he is not just an external presence but a presence dwelling within us. The Spirit helps us understnad the mind of Christ and the meaning of life. The Spirit helps us internalize worthy meanings, values, and intentions for life and empowers us to fulfill them. He makes Christ real to us!

We change in relationship to God at different levels. Many of us do and avoid doing specific things we believe God requires, such as obeying the Ten Commandments as life's basic rules. We work to gain God's favor and to avoid his wrath. We are being obedient to God's authority.

Some of us become even more Godlike by modeling our lives after the example of Christ as our perfect model. We incorporate more and more of his exemplary behavior into our own lives. We help the poor, we visit the sick, we love our neighbor.

Few of us, perhaps, internalize at the core of our being the Spirit of God so that everything we are and do is guided and energized by him—so that our lives show consistent evidence of the Spirit's work in us expressed in "love, joy, peace, patience, kindness, goodness, faithfulness, gentleness, self-control" (Gal. 5:22-23, RSV).

Compliance, identification, and internalization each has its place in learning and changing. But the changes we internalize have the most stable and enduring influence on our lives.

The Process of Changing

The changes we say yes to become a part of us. But they are not merely added like the parts of a jigsaw puzzle to form a whole picture. In a jigsaw puzzle, something is missing until the piece is added.

Some changes are like building an addition onto an

already-completed house—something is added not because it is missing but because what is there is not adequate.

Other changes are like rain; they come uninvited, bringing enrichment and refreshment or "spoiling our picnic."

Many changes require us to give up what now exists to put something new in its place, like removing old garments from the closet to make space for the new.

Life continues as is (unchanged), or life continues with additions and subtractions (change). Change is addition to and subtraction from what we already know, believe, feel, value, can do, and do.

Young children in their learning and growing process are primarily "adding to." But the older we get the more saying *yes* to change requires us to displace something old for something new. A lot of what we adults are involved in may be described as reeducation rather than education. We have to unlearn as well as learn! No wonder the older we get, the harder we sometimes find it to keep ourselves open to new ideas, opinions, experiences, and activities. This fact may have little to do with our capacity to continue learning and changing; it has everything to do with our willingness to do so. "Can I?" and "will I?" are two separate questions.

When we do decide to change, a process is set in motion. The process, as one person described it, involves "unfreezing, changing, and refreezing."[6] We have to thaw out or soften a stable condition in our lives which now exists; change the condition by replacing it, adding to it, or taking away from it; then refreeze the new condition—make it a firm part of us. Easier said than done!

The Southern Baptist Convention has a bold goal to share the gospel of Jesus Christ with every person in the world by the year 2000. No wonder *bold* is in the title of the denomination's theme, "Bold Mission Thrust." This goal, if accomplished, will require massive change in the denomination's missions strategy, substantive change in over thirty-five thousand Southern Baptist churches as they support missions at home and abroad, and significant changes in the lives of every church member who engages this gigantic task. In July, 1981, I read a news release quoting Dr. Dorothy Sample, newly-elected president of Woman's Missionary Union (Southern Baptist Convention). It read:

"For some Southern Baptists, Bold Mission Thrust has been a passive declaration without involvement," Dr. Sample said. "We must make a personal commitment and a bold response."

The WMU president described bold dreaming as visualizing what God can accomplish through women and bold vision as seeing the needs of the world.

"Bold living may mean giving up a job or career, living a more simple life-style, or giving up trivial things," she added.[7]

Consider what could happen if Dr. Sample's vision were lived out in just one area—missions giving.

At the present time only a small fraction of every dollar given by Southern Baptists is channeled through the Cooperative Program for worldwide missions. Just imagine what could happen if each church doubled its gifts for missions causes.

For this to happen a tradition that tends to support local causes at the expense of world missions would have to be unfrozen. Resistance to increased missions giving would have to be turned to support. Woman after woman and man after man would have to deal personally with what this means in her or his own life.

Putting the new condition in place would require many, many new things to happen in church stewardship education and commitment. Freezing (stabilizing) the new level of missions giving would take time.

The fact remains—change processes are difficult.

Unfreezing an attitude or behavior which is well in place is not easy; our motivation for change has to be strong enough to cause it to happen. In the case of Dr. Sample's suggestion, bold response to Christ's commission would have to break up barriers to certain giving patterns in many churches.

Changing, by putting a new condition in place, is demanding; we have to be able to decide on and believe in a new condition based on new information and experience. Implementing Dr. Sample's suggestion would require a fresh new interpretation and application of the Scriptures, among other things.

Even refreezing a change is not easy; it takes time to firm up a new condition as an established part of our lives so that it becomes as stable, well established, and accepted as the old condition. The process of changing is often difficult—in fact, so difficult at times it becomes impossible.

Deciding: The First Step to Change

Many of us chuckle at the following joke because we see ourselves in it. One person says to another: "Do you have trouble making decisions?"

The answer: "Yes and no."

Decision making is an exceedingly difficult task. Yet decision making is at the heart of change.

Mrs. William McMurry, "Mrs. Mac" as we lovingly called her, was one of the best decision makers I have ever known. We were on the staff of the Southern Baptist Woman's Missionary Union together. She was director of the Education Division in which I worked.

Mrs. Mac had the sensitivity, the wisdom, and the courage to say *yes* and *no* to change—to decide. She lived out of her commitment to high Christian ideals. She made deliberate choices, discerning God's leadership. She decided and concluded with diligent purposefulness. She took the best of the remembered past (history) and the best of the anticipated future (vision and hope) and blended them into purposeful action in the present. She saw meaning in current events, made commitments to issues and causes, willed change, and had the courage to act. But she did all of this with a sensitive appreciation for human relationships. Her keen intellect and strong will did not make her indifferent to others. She gave the gift of acceptance to everyone—even to people very different from her. She did not let disagreements and personal differences disburb the bonds of relationship between her and another person. She had integrity.

No wonder Mrs. Mac's daughter, Billie, commented about her mother, "She was true to her convictions and to herself and was therefore unable to be false to anyone."[8] Billie says a familiar piece of advice from her mother to her when she faced possible change—had a decision to make—and did not know which way to turn, was, "Billie, I can't see anything complicated about this at all. Simply do what you know is right in your heart, as far as your knowledge of the situation is concerned, and walk serenely amid the rubble, if rubble there need be."[9]

Our ability to decide is the crowning act of God's creation. He made us free by giving us the knowledge of truth. He made us responsible and invested trust in us. He made us capable of choice, expressing his belief in our highest possibilities. William James is quoted as saying, "The first act of freedom is to accept it." And when we do accept freedom responsibly, we pay great tribute to our Creator God.

While we often yearn for someone to give us neat, workable, pat answers to life, you and I would be the first to resist having someone else take away our freedom to decide by deciding for us. In the act of deciding, we exercise the unique human quality of will—the ability to decide, to choose, to conclude. God created us with the capacity for purposeful, deliberate, and intentional action. Exercising this gift, while scary, is a source of great joy in life.

Two couples, friends of mine, each have a new baby.

One couple planned for theirs, carefully scheduling their time of readiness for the added responsibility of parenting. In the case of the other parents, a birth control plan failed; pregnancy was the outcome. The planning for a child by one couple brought unfettered joy from the beginning. The other couple had to get through shock, disappointment, and grief to find joy. But they got there! They affirmed their capacity to be parents; they affirmed God's gift of new life; they reordered their short-range priorities as a family. In the end, by working through the crisis, they may have experienced even more joy in being parents to their child.

Sometimes we make decisions which determine our lives. At other times circumstances beyond our control determine our lives, leaving us only with the choice of how to relate to what is happening to us. In either case, choice is inevitable—decision is required.

No one of us—not even the best doctor in all the world—can control forever our loss of a loved one in death. But, once the grim fact of death occurs, we can decide how we will respond to the loss. You and I can choose the results we seek. Will I choose to live only with my past memories of life, allowing bitterness and discontent to cheat me of today and tomorrow? Or, will I choose to live today sustained by the memory of the gift of life and relationship I *have* enjoyed? And will I choose to be sustained by the hope that there will be other relationships I *will* enjoy as addition to and not subtraction from the earlier relationship? I cannot control my loss, but I can decide about the results I let it produce in my life.

Life is an endless chain of decisions, one after the other. We decide consciously or unconsciously to straighten out a relationship with a friend. We decide wisely or foolishly to spend money. We decide by deliberate choice or by default whether to stay in a present job. Even in not deciding, we decide, because the absence of a decision when one is needed constitutes a decision.

Making a Right Decision

"Do what you know is right" not only applies to the decisions we make but also to our ability to know a good decision when we see one. "What you know is right" implies that some guides for evaluation have been established (internalized). These guides help us sort out the bad from the good, the good from the better, the better from the best, and the most important from the least important.

What any one of us considers "right" can be arrived at from many starting points. The starting point or point of view is very important, then.

If I am thinking only of myself, I can ask: Is this change desirable, convenient, satisfying, pleasurable?

If I am thinking of how I fit into the groups of which I am a part, I can ask: Is this change fitting, appropriate, proper?

If I want to square my actions with the best knowledge available to me, I can ask: Is this change in accordance with fact, reason, or truth?

If I am concerned with meeting the demands of authority, I can ask: Does this change conform to expectations, rules, law, or policy?

If I am committed to God as the ultimate source of value, I can ask: Is this change helping me fulfill God's first and greatest commandment, "Thou shalt love the Lord thy God with all they heart, and with all thy soul, and with all thy mind . . . and . . . Thou shall love thy neighbour as thyself" (Matt. 22:37-39)?

In her last hours of terminal cancer, Mrs. Mac wrote four of her younger colleagues a letter. I was one of the four. Her last personal message to us was: "Man's approval is pleasant, but not essential." I believe her message was this: Pleasing God is the highest good; fulfilling his will is the highest achievement.

Mrs. Mac was the first person who helped me focus on decision making as a very serious challenge. Other people have, of course, influenced my thinking since then. Now, as a Christian, I believe:

- My ability to decide is God's imprint on me as a person created in his image. I can think, I can feel, I have a will with which to choose.
- Decisions are made by me through active choice and by default through not deciding.
- The quality of my decisions is only as good as the information on which the decisions are based. I need information from the past (history), present, and from my preferred future; I need data from my own experience and the experience of others; I need help from the ultimate source of wisdom—God— which I have in his Word and in his continuing revelation of himself to me and to others.
- The rightness of any decision has to be judged by how it will affect me, how it will affect others, and how it will affect the mission I share with God in the world.[10]
- Everyday moments of decision are the "crossing points"[11] where God and I are most likely to meet. Decision times are the intersections where the meaning of the gospel and the meaning of my own experience meet.
- The first step in change is to decide and do the things I already know are right for me and others in my world in light of God's intention for us. "Faith is walking to the edge of all the light I have and taking one more step."[12] As I do God's will—the part of it I already know—he reveals more of it to me.

Crossing Points in Decision and Change

An experience in the life of Moses illustrates a crossing point, a point of decision and change. "One day as Moses was tending the flock of his father-in-law . . . suddenly the Angel of Jehovah appeared to him as a flame of fire in a bush. When Moses saw that the bush was on fire and that it didn't burn up, he went over to investigate. Then God called out to him" (Ex. 3:1-5, TLB).

Moses was going about his daily business when a dramatic incident caught his attention. While Moses took care of the ordinary task of tending sheep, God got Moses' attention and called him to mission. The place became the holy ground of a meeting between God and man—a place of decision and change.

In the aftermath of a tornado in Louisville, Kentucky, in April of 1974, I saw God working at points where human need met the meaning of the gospel. Students of The Southern Baptist Theological Seminary spontaneously organized search parties for tornado victims, operated food and emergency clothing services for dislocated persons, and worked quietly among people trying to help them put life back together again.

Gospel meanings were abundantly clear against the backdrop of disaster. Human life is sacred. "Bear ye one another's burdens" and "Give to persons in need" were alive as belief-in-practice. The words of Christ had heightened meaning in the midst of personal doing of the Word, "Inasmuch as ye have done it unto one of the least of these my brethren, ye have done it unto me" (Matt. 25:40). A disaster brought a decision to act out the gospel in these unusual circumstances.

A decision point happened for a foreign missionary who stopped one night in the 1960s in front of a closed drive-in restaurant. In stopping to rest, he looked up to see these words scrawled across a plate-glass window, "We don't serve niggers." His experience that night crossed at a new level with the meaning of the gospel. He made a deeper level decision that God's mission in the world required him to serve any person who is in need of God's salvation, love, or care. He made this decision at a time when many people were having trouble expressing Christian care and love across the barrier of race. The ground in front of a closed drive-in restaurnat became the holy ground of encounter between God and a person. And out of it, a commitment to missions was deepened—changed.

Life has a lot of intersections where choice is not only possible but also unavoidable. Shall I go straight? Turn left? Turn right? Take one step? Take three steps? Return to start? Say yes? Say no? You and I must decide.

In these moments we are most likely to find God at work with us. In these moments his Spirit speaks to us, nudges us, supports us, guides us, give us wisdom to decide. "The wisdom we speak of is that mysterious secret wisdom of God which he planned before the creation. . . . Not using the expressions of the human intellect but those which the Holy Spirit teaches us, explaining things to those who are spiritual" (1 Cor. 2:7,13, Phillips).

The Easier Yes

There are conditions which tend to make it easier for us to say yes to change. When these conditions are present, we are more likely to make and keep our commitments to change. Some of these conditions are: readiness; match of new conditions with existing habits and norms; adequate time allowance; capacity for independent action; and support for change. We will explore these one by one to help us better understand why it is sometimes more difficult and sometimes easier to change.

1. *Readiness.* As children, most of us played games of hide-and-seek. In my neighborhood, the seeker was called "It." With eyes tightly closed, "It" counted to ten, then called out loudly, "Here I come, ready or not." Change possibilities are a little like this. They search us out "ready or not," often as impersonally as an "it." But, even more important, we sometimes search out change possibilities because we are ready. Wherever the initiative occurs, change comes when the opportunity for change and our readiness for change connect.

Sometimes readiness for change is present in us. Sometimes change forces from outside bring us to the just-right moment for saying yes.

Sometimes the . . . factors are within: a burst of inexplicable courage that propels us beyond real or imagined barriers, a sudden surge of energy, a bold idea, a spontaneous decision to act, the welling up and overflowing of faith, hope, and love. Usually we surprise even ourselves in these moments. Sometimes the forces are exterior: Someone, maybe a friend or a mentor, forces us to dig deeper than we ever would have on our own and helps us to discover resources we have never dreamed we had. Or it may be a cataclysmic event—a death that shakes us to our boots, a traumatic loss, a disaster that tumbles down walls and reveals new avenues of possibilities. Other times it is something simple . . . a word or an embrace, a gorgeous sunset, a phrase that speaks directly and healingly to a deep need. More often, it is a combination of people, events, and happenings that help us out of a rut and set us on a swift new course.[13]

"Ready" is such a good feeling. 10, 9, 8, 7, 6, 5, 4, 3, 2, 1, go! The state of being ready implies willingness, availability, and preparedness for action.

Natural readiness for change tends to diminish the older we get. Discovery of new possibilities gradually gives way to repetition of existing ways. Building of relationships, of families, and careers gives way to maintenance. And properly so. Effective maintenance of what we have built in life is as important as the original process of building. Perhaps it should not surprise us as adults that a lot of change for us—and readiness for change—relates to maintaining what we have already built.

We understand maintenance of a house or an appliance. We add a new roof to a house, oil an appliance, replace a part in a lamp. Maintenance of life is similar—repairing damage, correcting dysfunction, adjusting, replacing parts, rebuilding. Life situations change. At these change points, we often experience great needs to learn, and these needs bring us some of the most "teachable moments" in our lives.

Even as we grow older, life is not all maintenance. It also is new construction. A new dream. A new thought. A new commitment. A new relationship. The possibility of new dimensions in life is unending, although it may be diminished by age or interrupted by crises. We have unending capacity for new experiences in life if we stay open to them.

Recently I visited with Allen Graves, retired dean of the School of Religious Education at The Southern Baptist Theological Seminary in Louisville, Kentucky, He told me about the experiences he and his wife, Helen, had in teaching at the Baptist seminary in Nigeria in the first two years after his formal retirement from teaching in the states.

I asked Dr. Graves, "How did you adapt what you know to the unique needs of Nigerians?" He smiled broadly and his eyes danced with excitement.

"I had to work at it," he said, "but I may have done some of the best teaching in my lifetime." Then he explained his technique of visiting and observing church work in the Nigerian setting. He shared his experiences in training students to write their own case studies which brought their experiences right into the classroom for study. He told me about a plan he called "eureka reports" in which students reported weekly the highlights of what they were reading and what they were experiencing as ministers-in-training. He adapted (changed) his teaching methods to the new situation.

I sensed that in his retirement, Allen Graves was still pushing into new frontiers of theological education. I wasn't surprised. I reflected on his influence in my own life as my major professor when I was a doctoral student, as my dean when I was a teacher, and as my co-worker when later we worked together as administrators in the same institution. More than any other one person, he supported and encouraged me in my studies of change processes. And why not? He obviously fully intended to be involved in change processes the rest of his life.

Mark, a young man I work with, has a talented artist mother who didn't start painting until she was fifty-eight years old. She now both teaches art and paints. A beautiful painting of a field of Texas bluebonnets by Anna King hangs in my office, reminding me that life always holds the possibility of newness.

When Gene Chamberlain, another co-worker of mine told me one Monday morning, "I rode a water sked this weekend," the telltale signs of pleasure—and sunburn—were on his face.

"A what?" I asked.

My impression from his description is that water skedding is similar to water skiing, except one sits on a sked rather than standing on skis. Anyway, I was appropriately impressed at the bravery of this man in his fifties.

My curiosity was not satisfied. "What caused you to try this new thing?" I asked.

"It came easy," Gene explained. "My wife and I were at the lake with friends. A friend asked me, 'Do you want to try?' He invited me and encouraged me, but he didn't press. Almost before I knew it I said, 'Yes, I want to try.' "

He tried. He succeeded!

Whatever the circumstances, and at whatever age forces converge to make us ready for something new; these create times of readiness. When readiness is present, change is easier.

2. *Match of New Conditions with Existing Values and Norms.* When a new experience matches or is in agreement with values or norms which already exist, changing is easier. For example, the dominant norms of our culture support the marriage relationship as a context for birthing and rearing children. For Christians, marriage is viewed as the normative context for parenting. Therefore, changing to a parent role by adopting a child usually is easier for a married couple than for a single adult.

What an individual values personally is of ultimate importance to that person. What a group values collectively comes to be considered normative for that group. Our personal values are central beliefs which control our personal behavior. Group norms are basic expectations about behavior which control behavior of members of the group.

Personal values and group norms are means of conserving what is most important to us—individually and as a group. Conserving means protecting things of great significance from deterioration or loss—change.

Values and norms are powerful forces. They are strong constraints against change which runs counter to them. They are strong forces for change which is compatible with them. They serve the valuable function of preserving what an individual or group considers valuable enough to conserve. Once in place, values and norms both resist and support change.

If the Great Commission of Christ to share the gospel with the whole world has meaning and value to me, it is easier for me to increase (change) my offering to missions or to increase the time I spend in mission action in my own community.

If it is normative for women to work outside the home in my culture, changing into a "working mother" is easier.

If it is normative in my denomination for men only to be ordained as pastors and deacons, ordaining a man is much easier for my church than ordaining a woman.

We can expect change which is consistent with dominant values and norms to be easier than changes which "runs against the tide."

At the point of values and norms, we Christians have some of our greatest struggles. As human beings, we have great possibilities for good and for evil. As we try to internalize God's ultimate values as modeled by Christ, we struggle with lesser values—like how to experience *agape* love as well as love in purely human terms and how to have faith in God which puts faith in self in perspective. Changing to Godlikeness is difficult because it is easy to settle for purely human values. This difficulty is compounded when we are a part of a culture in which Christian commitment and aspirations are not normative. It is much easier to become a Christian and grow in the Christian life within a family or community of believers (church) where Christian values are cherished and where Christian commitment is normative. For this very reason, the family unit and the church fellowship are strategic in God's plan for us.

---

3. *Adequate Time Allowance.* Change tends to be easier when we have time to adjust to it. "Give me time" can be a delay tactic for putting off change as long as possible—or forever. But "give me time" also can signal a healthy need for time to adjust. Adjustment to and internalization of change take time. Generally, change is easier when it is accompanied by a reasonable time allowance for adjustment.

If a house gets destroyed by a tornado, we understand that it takes time to repair or rebuild the house. We allow time for the rebuilding to happen. Sometimes we are not as aware that it takes even more time to rebuild the relationship structure of a family or a marriage which has been changed by death, by birth, by absence, or by illness. What constitutes "adequate" time is individual to each of us.

In my growing-up years, I remember hearing this kind of comment by adults: "Ben seems interested in Betty, but surely he couldn't be—his wife has been dead only six months." I got a distinct impression as a child listening to adult conversation that at least one year of adjustment time was normative before one should consider remarriage after the death of a spouse. This is an example of a group honoring a norm which supported time to adjust to the death of a spouse. The unwritten rule was: It is inappropriate to consider remarriage after the death of a spouse for at least a year. "Why" probably got lost for many people along the way. But this norm—whether the time factor was too little or too much—served the purpose of supporting a period of time for adjustment. A group of people understood that change and adjustment to change take time.

Change is easier when there is an adequate allowance for adjustment.

4. *Capacity for Independent Action.* Change also is easier in areas of our lives in which we can take more independent action. If a change primarily affects only me, I have some capacity for independent action. Change is easier in this case. I can decide and do some things without taking the time to involve someone else.

The more interdependent we are with others, however, the more difficult change is because more than one person needs to be directly involved in a decision to change. A single person can decide to take a new job and move to a new location much easier than a married person with teenage children. The more persons there are directly affected by the decision, the more difficult the decision is to make in terms of time and energy.

Capacity for independent action does not mean it is easier to make a right decision, only that it is easier to make a decision.

Once we get a decision in place, it is often difficult for us to be patient with other persons who also must decide. Independent decision making is much easier and much less time consuming. This is why a "boss"—even though time would allow—announces rather than consults, commands rather that guides. This is why parents in dealing with children often tell without explaining and announce with a no-questions-asked stance. It appears easier to change through independent decision making than through group decision or group influence on decision.

Recently I announced to employees who work with me some conclusions I was beginning to reach. Because I am supervisor, even a strong suggestion can be heard as a decision. Silence spread over the room—an uncomfortable, stifling silence. Then one employee, who had told us earlier that one way he deals with too much pressure and tension is to take a brisk walk, said, "If we do what you've just suggested, I will have to take a very long walk!" Laughter broke the tension as I commented, "But will you come back from the walk?" Then we talked about the tentative conclusions I had reached.

My conclusions were heading us in the right direction; that was not the problem. What was happening was that as soon as I got a sense of direction, I wanted a lot of things we were doing to be changed to support that direction—immediately. Nothing was wrong with that either on the surface! What was bothering the employees was my expectation to have things happen too fast for our team to implement them. We needed more information to know how to handle the details of change. We needed time to test ideas, to adapt plans, to adjust thinking and schedules.

Changing is easier when we can do it independently; but when we change conditions for others close to us by our independent action, the "ease" is lost. When people seriously affected by a decision—especially negatively—do not have opportunity to be heard in the decision-making process, they force us to deal with them in the process of implementing a decision. Grousing, foot-dragging, and sabotaging of plans are expressions of continuing resistance. Any time saved in making a quicker decision on the front end is more than lost in the process of group implementation of the decision.

This dynamic explains why many parents and supervisors are sometimes efficient decision makers without being effective ones. They can make relatively quick and good decisions, but they have trouble getting decisions implemented effectively. Efficient decisions often become ineffective decisions in achieving the results being sought. The efficiency of the decision is lost in enormous expenditures of time, energy, and money in the implementation stage.

Deciding alone is easier, but this ease can be claimed only when there is no significant impact on others affected by the decision.

5. *Support for Change.* Perhaps the most crucial factor in change is the support we feel for changing. Support comes from our own values, from norms of groups to which we belong, from our relationship with God, and from our relationship with other people significant to us. Changing against a tide of support has to happen—like doing something we know is right even when it is not the

popular thing to do. But when we feel the buoying support from other persons important to us, change is much, much easier. This point is discussed further in the chapter titled, "Reducing the Costs of Change."

As persons we are planted firmly in our world—our world of family, church, work, community, national boundary, and international concern. In these worlds we are free to make whatever decisions we will, to say yes and no to change. The burden of our freedom to decide and to change is awesome and unending. In the oratorio, *What Is Man?* are these words:

> My mark—God made it—
>   My mark is freedom.
> God made it, never to be taken, else I'd be not man.
>   Its burden is endless, sometimes bitter,
>   but it is mine forever.
> Turn me not back from the sky
>   But light me a star in the dark self.[14]

God who gives the freedom to decide is the same one who lights our path for decisive living—for saying yes and no to change.

For Your Reflection

1. Think back to some of the changes in your life. Can you think of specific instances in which you changed at different levels?

    (1) Can you recall a change you made because someone in authority required you to change (compliant change)?

    (2) Can you recall changes you made because an attractive model(s) demonstrated an alternative way of thinking, feeling, looking, or doing, and gave you a pattern to follow (identification change)?

    (3) Can you recall changes you made in your life which are very firmly in place because they

have deep personal meaning and significance to you (internalized change)?

(4) Can you recall some instances where your first change was compliant but later came to be internalized by you as something important to you and not just somebody else's idea?

(5) Which level of change do you tend to be most comfortable with?

2. What is your experience of changing in your relationship to God? Does your experience cause you to agree or disagree with the three paragraphs on page 59?

3. Which of the following questions most often guide you in decision making?

(1) Is this action desirable, convenient, satisfying, pleasurable?

(2) Is this action fitting, appropriate, proper?

(3) Is this action in accordance with fact, reason, or truth?

(4) Does this action conform to expectation of others, rules, laws, or policies?

(5) Is what I am about to do helping me fill God's first and greatest commandment, "Thou shalt love the Lord thy God with all thy heart, and with all thy soul, and with all thy strength . . . and thy neighbour as thyself"?

4. Study the author's statement of belief about decision making on page 66. What would you change in this statement? Write your own statement or edit the author's statement to become yours.

5. Think about one change you want very much to see happen in your family or church. Evaluate the relative ease or difficulty of making the change based on some of the conditions which make change easier. If you can answer yes to any one of the questions below, this indicates change would tend to be easier than if the answer is no:

(1) Is there readiness for change?

(2) Is the change in harmony with existing values and norms?

(3) Is adequate time being allowed to make the change?
(4) Are the people most affected by the change participating in these decisions about the change?
(5) Is there support for changing?

5

God, infuse into me the spirit
of adventure. Through the
blinding haze of reluctance
I catch a vision of a new
tomorrow.

—Billie Pate

5
Resisting Change

"Changing is about as difficult as scaling a vertical cliff."—a person trying to change his marriage for the better.

"I know I am headed in the right direction, but it seems like a sixty mph head wind is holding me back."—a person trying to simplify an affluent life-style to make room for expressing concern in a world where millions of people are starving.

"I don't understand myself at all, for I really want to do what is right, but I can't. I do what I don't want to—what I hate. . . . When I want to do good, I don't; and when I try not to do wrong, I do it anyway"—the apostle Paul (Rom. 7:15,19, TLB).

How do persons in bondage gain freedom? How is a drab house turned into a place of beauty? How does a person without knowledge learn? How do enemies become brothers? How do children mature? How does a person encapsulated in grief break out to fullness of life again?

Change. Between bondage and freedom is change. Between drabness and beauty (ask the butterfly) is change—painful, difficult, struggling change. For change to occur, resistance to change has to be confronted. No wonder we sometimes perceive the path to change to be one step forward and two steps backward before we can move forward again. No wonder Paul, in identifying a strong resistance in himself and sensing limits in changing, affirmed, "I thank God there is a way out through Jesus Christ our Lord" (Rom. 7:25, Phillips).

Resistance to change is as necessary as change itself. Saying no is an important option. No signals a negative response—refusal, denial, disagreement about, opposition to, not being ready for, or fear of an alternate being considered. Our capacity to say no emerges early in life. Even a two-year-old has *no* in his vocabulary. Beginning at an early age and continuing through adolesence into adulthood, no is a response to be cultivated and used appropriately.

We assert who we are through the nos and yeses of our lives. What we say no to, as well as what we say yes to, molds our lives, shapes our characters, influences our health and well being, and establishes the quality of our lives. In saying no to smoking, for example, a health hazard is avoided. No creates a positive outcome. In saying no to training, we may limit our work opportunities. No creates a negative outcome.

Saying no has positive or negative consequences in shaping life. The resistance forces within us and among us can save us from destructive change, but they can also hold us back from constructive change. Wisdom is knowing the difference.

Saying No

There are many, many ways we prepare ourselves to say no to change—to resist. These preparations are the healthy and unhealthy defenses we build against change. Our defenses are healthy to the extent they are strong enough to protect us against unnecessary or hurtful change but open enough to allow us to let in constructive change. Our resistance to change is unhealthy when we become tightly closed to all new possibilities.

The following are some of the more powerful resistance structures we build and use against change: habits and norms, selective listening, dependence on early models and tradition, the sacrosanct, vested interests, and suspicion of outsiders.[1]

1. *Habits and Norms.* —These are two powerful resistance forces to change. Habits are personal—they are the automatic, familiar, and preferred ways we do things, put in place by repetition. We become attached to our routines, like always taking a nap on Sunday afternoon or going home at Christmas time. We begin unconsciously to feel that whatever is perpetuated through habit is good, and whatever breaks habit is bad.

Norms develop in groups in the same ways habits do in individuals. They are customary and expected ways of behaving within a group. Norms control behavior as groups come to hold certain unwritten expectations about such things as dress, language, levels of intimacy, and lifestyle. When a group member violates a group norm, resistance to the change can be intense within the group.

2. *Selective listening.* —another resistance against change is selective listening. Our tendency is to hear only what we want to hear. We receive new information and experiences through filters which remove threatening or unpleasant messages. We give words the meanings we want them to have. How do you think a husband hears "uh-huh" when his wife responds this way to his question, "Does it create any problem for you if I go fishing today?"

When you or I hear the phrase "equal rights for women," it can mean anything from more freedom, to equal pay for equal work, to destruction of the traditional family, to blurring of differences between male and female. How we are prepared to listen makes the difference. We often hear a new term or idea as reinforcing an original belief or value of ours when the speaker or writer meant to give us information quite different in meaning.

During a banquet conversation one night, I listened to a friend report the move of an employee from a position in another department to her department. "Have you heard Jane Smith is moving up to a position in our department?"

she asked. Knowing the transfer was a lateral one, and not a promotion, my first impulse was to think Jane was moving up to a new floor in the building. That interpretation didn't work, however, because the move would be down to another floor. Then it hit me—my friend valued her own department more than the other department. Her bias colored her perception of what was happening. To her, the lateral transfer was a promotion for Jane.

When I pointed out what she said, my friend was shocked. She was unaware of the message she had delivered. She had selectively listened to the information about Jane's transfer and heard what she wanted to hear.

Jesus may have been dealing with the problem of selective listening in asking Peter three times, "Do you love me?" (John 21:15). He needed Peter to understand the meanings in his question which were deeper than Peter was prepared to hear. He knew Peter could selectively listen to the love question in human terms only. Jesus needed him to understand divine love, the only love adequate to sustain him in fulfilling his vocation in life.

3. *Models and tradition.* —We resist a lot of change because of our dependence on early models and tradition. All of us go through life highly dependent on persons who influenced us early in life. Even in adulthood we tend to agree more than we disagree with our parents and early teachers on such basic points as religion, politics, and child rearing. Dependence on early models is strong, as is dependence on tradition. A person, for example, keeps her membership in the Presbyterian church because her family is traditionally Presbyterian. Or a person registers as a Republican, as did his father and his grandfather. Or a person farms exactly like his dad whether or not there are now better ways to farm.

Our insecurities and fears in the present often cause us to seek security in the structures and traditions we have inherited from the past. When life grows difficult and frustrating, we look with nostalgia to "the good ol' days." We resist the emerging new by clinging to the past.

Our inheritance often is good, something to be conserved, but we may need to be reminded:

Instead of giving . . . the impression that . . . (our) task is to stand a dreary watch over ancient values, we must keep telling ourselves the bracing truth that it is [our] task to recreate these values continuously in [our] own behavior, facing the dilemmas and catastrophies in our time. Instead of implying . . . the ideas we cherish are safely embalmed in the memory of old battles and ancestral deeds we should be telling [ourselves] that each generation refights the crucial battles and brings a new vitality to the old ideals or allows them to decay.[2]

Our tendency to overdepend on our inheritance is noted in the Bible. We are admonished not only to put our faith into words which conserve meaning from generation to generation but also to live the words in deed. "Love must not be a matter of words or talk; it must be genuine, and show itself in action" (1 John 3:18, NEB). Each new generation must discover meaning and value and appropriate it personally.

4. *The sacrosanct.*—Another resistance force to change is whatever we make sacrosanct by elevating it to a position of sacred. We give some things a sacred quality although they are not intrinsically sacred. Some things become our "sacred cows". Whatever is considered sacred—genuine or not—becomes relatively immune to change. The US flag. Nationalism. The doxology sung on Sunday morning.

We create forms to express meaning and value. Sometimes we elevate what we have created to a special position of reverence or immunity to change. In these cases, humanity's creation becomes sacrosanct, as the King James Version of the Bible is to some Christians—the version itself, in addition to the central truth of the Bible, is made sacred. In some churches the 11:00 AM hour of Sunday morning worship is sacrosanct—the hour itself rather than what happens during it is inviolable. Whatever we elevate to the status of sacred becomes highly resistant to change.

---

5. *Vested interests.* — Our vested interests cause us to resist change. Over periods of time, persons and groups invest vast amounts of time, energy, and money in endeavors, as Moses did in leading the children of Israel out of bondage. When this happens, there is a natural tendency to keep feeling solely responsible for the effort. Vested interests are good in the sense that they affirm our ability to commit to and invest in causes. Loyalty to commitments is a quality to be admired. But vested interests are bad when they blind us to the help we need from others. For example, a leader may have almost single-handedly developed a new organization. As the organization grows, leadership needs to be shared but the original investor has trouble sharing the leadership with someone else. It took Jethro to help Moses relinquish one-man rule and build an organization with capacity to serve the needs of the children of Israel.

As we invest in any endeavor, certain benefits begin to accrue to us, such as position, prestige, wealth, and power. We often feel a stronger and stronger need to protect our investment.

Children can become vested interests of parents who invest years of nurture, guidance, support, and care in them during the childhood years. Parents sometimes have trouble "giving up" children when it is time for them to move from home and establish lives of their own.

6. *Suspicion of outsiders.* — We resist change through our basic suspicion or distrust of outsiders. The biggest threat to us is that we will be changed by a person or group of persons different from us. The stranger, the "different one," is usually suspect.

The entrance of a new leader from outside an organization creates a potential for great change within the organization; the new leader's ideas are often suspect.

A person in training session comments, "That's a good idea, but it won't work in our situation. We're different."

Jesus was a stranger, as you recall, to the religious

establishment of his day. He was suspect; then he was rejected completely as the ultimate defense against change.

Differences between people are a major source of creative change possibility. Because of this, differences also are the greatest barriers between people. This point is so pivotal to understanding change, an entire chapter is given to it titled "Listening to Strangers."

The means we use to resist change are varied. These illustrations help us understand some of the sources of the resistance we experience. Hopefully, they help us appreciate the value of resistance as well as the pitfalls of it. The things mentioned—habits and norms, selective listening, dependence on early models and tradition, the sacrosanct, vested interests, and suspicion of outsiders—are all rooted in what we have already said yes to. When we say no, we do it to protect what is comfortable or what is valuable to us. The burden is on us to know whether we are defending something valuable enough to defend or merely something comfortable.

Recognizing Resistance

The signs of resistance are more easily recognized once we know what to look for in ourselves and in others. Listening to our conversations often gives us some of our biggest clues. Here are but a few of the more popular expressions of resistance:

"What we are doing works, why tamper with it?"

"If it was good enough for dad, it is good enough for me."

"I couldn't change it if I wanted to."

"If things were only the way they were when . . ."

"Yes, but . . ."

"We just don't do things that way."

That's a good idea, but it won't work for me."

"But everybody's doing it."

"We can't . . ."

"We won't . . ."

"It isn't in our/my best interest to . . ."

"It isn't right to . . ."

Resistance can also be seen as well as heard by the sensitive person. I remember walking into a room for a first meeting with a new group I would be supervising. Although I had had a one-to-one interview with every person before the meeting, there were signs of some tension in the room—a very natural thing for a new group and a new leader even when they feel good about being brought together.

One person in the group was obviously resisting the new relationship. He was seated in a chair at the end of the table opposite from me. His chair was tipped back against the wall, his hands were folded across his chest, and part of the time his eyes were closed, as if to deny what was happening was really happening. Fortunately, this was a temporary resistance which passed in a short time.

Silence and withdrawal often signal resistance. On the other extreme, boisterous talk and overreacting to what is said or done can indicate resistance. Keeping busy to avoid thinking about what is happening is another technique for avoiding (resisting) what is new.

Responding to Resistance

We are called on to deal with the resistance we personally feel toward change as well as with resistance other people express toward change. Three guidelines can help us do this:

Expect resistance as both natural and desirable.
Listen to resistance to understand it.
Take resistance seriously and learn from it.

Much simpler said than done! In discussing these three points, we will focus on resistance we are able to spot in other people rather than the resistance we can find within ourselves. This more objective viewpoint makes it easier to learn. We then can apply what we learn to our personal, more subjective experiences with resistance.

1. *Expect resistance as both natural and desirable.* Remember, it takes both change and resistance to change to create equilibrium in life. Our need for stability *and* change means we must defend ourselves against unnecessary or harmful change. Resistance can be thought of as a useful red flag, a signal that something important is about to happen which can have harmful as well as beneficial consequences.

Sometimes we are more able to grant ourselves permission to feel resistance than to grant others the right to it. Whatever I resist or defend tends to be automatically reasonable, rational, and realistic. Whatever others resist or defend, if different from my position, is unreasonable, irrational, and unrealistic. This may or may not be true. Resistance is much more easily dealt with when we anticipate it ahead of time—know it probably is going to be there. Anticipating resistance takes away some of the shock of "bumping into it in the dark." Seeing it as natural, and even desirable, makes the pain of it easier to bear.

Resistance is built into the fabric of life processes. A young child enters the world totally dependent. At about eighteen months to two years of age, the child begins to get capacity for some independence. *No* becomes a key word in his vocabulary. No wonder "the terrible twos" is a phrase sometimes used to describe the developmental stage when a young child first resists parental authority and conducts early experiments with his own capacities for limited independence.

Adolescence is another human development period in which resistance is dramatically evident. During the teen years, a person moves from childhood (dependence) to adulthood (interdependence). But life does not flow in a straight line from dependence to interdependence. To be interdependent with others, we must first experience what it means to be independent—to have a clear sense of identity and worth as a unique person. The mature adult relationship combines the God-given capacities for dependence and independence. It takes both!

Adolescents suffer greatly, as do the parents of adolescents, as they struggle to assert their independence. To do this, adolescents resist parental authority and influence. Parents are wrong; the teenager is right. Teenagers see the world from a newly independent frame of reference. Adolescents tend to value what their peers think, believe, and feel above what adults think, believe, and feel.

Parents often experience deep resistance, even temporary rejection, by their children as they pass through the adolescent years. Even when adolescence is understood as the natural growth phase it is, there is still pain. But when adolescent resistance is not anticipated and understood by parents, it can be even more of a problem to the parent-child relationship.

Balancing dependence and independence continues to be a struggle throughout our lives. Sometimes we must resist excessive independence because it cuts us off from relationships which support and sustain us. Sometimes we must say no to excessive dependence.

I have watched my parents, now in their seventies, work to balance independence and dependence in new ways. As we children have planned with them to help them take care of themselves and adjust their living arrangements to meet their changed needs, we have been aware of their needs for as much independence as they can possibly maintain. Our stated family goal is to help them be as independent as possible for as long as possible. They have every right to resist unnecessary dependence. By expecting resistance of unnecessary dependence by our parents and by listening to it, we children may be able to make a more sensitive response to our parents' needs.

In similar fashion, we can know to expect people to resist change for the reasons we have discussed, plus others. If we are prepared to discover both the capacity to change and the capacity to resist change, we will not be totally surprised by resistance in others or in ourselves. Accepting resistance as natural prepares us to listen to it.

2. *Listening to resistance to understand it.* Listening to resistance is never easy. Our ears pick up the *yeses* we are looking for. *Yes, yes sir,* and *yes ma'am* are pleasant to hear. No is so difficult to deal with, we sometimes take precaution to shield ourselves from saying or hearing it.

Nos are sometimes difficult to say right. They are subject to being said too soon or too late. On one hand, we make a suggestion and encounter a barrage of words about why the suggestion won't work—an immediate no which leaves almost no room to search for the yes possibility. On the other hand, we make a suggestion and encounter a stated yes or maybe—only to find out later, after too much investment of time and energy, that the person really wanted to say *no* all along. We might like to blame these persons for the problems they create for us, but blaming will not change them.

I recently saw the "difficult no" working between my sister and brother-in-law and their fifteen-year-old teenager. In his wallet John had a brand new learner's permit for driving. For weeks he had talked to me about a trip he and his family would take during his spring break from school. When I heard his parents talk about this same trip, they said something like "John wants to go. . . . " I sensed no commitment to the trip on the parents' part, only a lingering maybe.

The dream of the trip was very alive in the mind of John. Vacation approached. Bonnie, a younger sister, got a surprise vacation trip to Florida with a friend. The need for his own trip and the anticipated experience of driving the car, intensified for John. He was doing yard work for me during the early part of his vacation week, and at the end of each day he would say, "I'll be out of town after Thursday."

I would reply, "Fine, there is work to do here all week, but I understand the trip comes first."

SAY NO, SAY YES TO CHANGE

This situation persisted until Thursday when John reported, "We aren't taking a trip." He didn't say more, but he obviously was disappointed.

Were John's parents at fault for "stringing" him along until the last minute when a no could no longer be avoided? Or was John at fault for not picking up the resistance signals of his parents and dealing with these? Without placing blame, we can conclude they both were caught in the problem of saying and hearing a no.

A beneficial skill we can learn is to listen to no and maybe for what they are—whether they are spoken softly, almost imperceptibly, or clearly. Even when it is not what we want to hear, we can learn to receive no messages for what they are.

When we encounter resistance we too soon let it become something to be ignored or overcome. And, if we get too busy too early overcoming resistance, we may never understand its message and meaning. We must keep reminding ourselves that resistance signals something new or different is about to happen—change. This something, this new event or condition, can be beneficial or harmful to everyone concerned.

The possibility of the harmful/hurtful outcome is what brings out the no. The possibility of a beneficial outcome is what brings out the yes. The yes threatens the no; the no threatens the yes. In these circumstances, our first tendency is to overcome or put down the opposing force.

As leaders, parents, and friends, we have special techniques for dealing with resistance in others. Some of the techniques we use with others are giving unsought advice, premature persuading, censoring, controlling, and punishing. These techniques may eventually need to be used. But, if used too soon, they create a situation in which more complete understanding between two people is thwarted. Better to save these techniques as last-resort measures under the label "for emergency use only."

The most productive response to resistance is to listen to it in order to understand it. If we shift too quickly into the advising, persuading, controlling, punishing mode, we may never learn what we need to learn from the no or the maybe. Listening to understand does not even require a maybe or a tentative yes. Listening requires a suspended judgment until more of the facts are in (they are almost never *all* in).

Listening to understand before passing judgment is a skill which requires great inner strength and discipline. One of the greatest gifts one person can give another, however, is understanding. My life and yours have been enriched by persons who cared enough about us to try to understand us before judging what we say or do. As I write this book, I can pay tribute to my division director, Bill Graham, who has a remarkable capacity to hear and understand his employees, including me.

Understanding does not require agreement. Understanding does not require acceptance of the other point of view. But understanding does require seeing things from another person's perspective, knowing so well what the other person is saying that we can clearly state the person's case for him. Understanding another person communicates to that person that we take him seriously and that we are open to learning about or from his different point of view.

3. *Take resistance seriously and learn from it.* If we pay the price to understand resistance, we can learn from it. The price is concern for the other person, respect for another's point of view, and fairness in dealing with a point of view different from our own. Understanding precedes judging. What appears negative on the surface may or may not be upon a closer look. But, more important, understanding precedes judging because if we must eventually disagree, we do it against a backdrop of understanding.

"Do unto others as you would have them do unto you" seems relevant. If someone needs to give us advice for our own good, censure us for unacceptable action, persuade us to take an alternative course of action, or even punish us, we take this a little better knowing the other person understands our point of view. When we turn the tables, the requirement is to give the same treatment to the other person.

Several years ago my sister and her family were visiting me. While we adults chatted inside the house, the older children—John and Bonnie—aged seven and five then played in the backyard with a putting iron and golf balls. They were joined by their eighteen-month-old brother, Greg, who obviously was an interruption and bother to their play. Soon John came in to report that Greg was tearing up my tomato plants along the fence. He made a dramatic plea for help. My sister said, "Watch him and keep him away from the plants." Not much more time passed before John dragged Greg into the house with another report that Greg would not leave the tomato plants alone.

I walked outside with Greg. Sure enough, he moved straight toward the plants. He resisted our efforts to keep him away from them. But as I followed him trying to figure out the attraction of the tomato plants, I got the picture from Greg's point of view. On the other side of the fence, beyond the tomato plants in the yard next door, was an attractive sandbox filled with all kinds of interesting toys. He couldn't care less about the tomato plants—the sandbox was what mattered! He was resisting our efforts to keep him away from the tomato plants because what he really wanted was to get beyond the tomato plants to the sandbox. Understanding things from his point of view brought a whole new understanding to the situation.

When we listen to resistance signals, we get insight into reasons for the resistance. Some of these reasons are ones that we can do something about, like getting permission for Greg to play in the sandbox in the yard next door. Here are but a few of the important messages we can pick up and do something about in listening to resistance.

Resistance can signal that the purpose of change and

the results of change are not clearly understood by the persons involved. In this case, the purpose and anticipated results need to be clarified.

Resistance can disclose inadequate communication and insufficient flow of information. In the face of inadequate information, persons tend to resist on the basis of misinformation or no information. More and better information often helps.

Resistance can bring about a closer scrutiny of the ultimate consequences of change, both immediate and long-range. Sometimes the first steps of change seem clear and harmless but the ultimate consequences are not in view. Sometimes the opposite condition exists—the short-range pitfalls are so evident that longer-range benefits are obscured. Dealing objectively with short-range and longer-range consequences can reduce resistance or validate resistance as appropriate.

Resistance can signal inadequate problem-solving and decision-making processes. People tend to be lazy and apathetic toward objectives which are not their own. Lack of involvement of persons in decisions which affect them precipitates resistance simply because the persons weren't involved. Increasing participation and involvement often helps.

When resistance is present, it can be dealt with more creatively when it is expressed, heard, and understood before it is either accepted or challenged.

For Your Reflection

1. Identify some potential changes which are likely to happen in your life in the next few years which you feel a need to resist. (They may be in you, in your family, in your school system, in your church, or in your work setting.) List them.

    (1) On a scale from 1 to 10 (1 is low and 10 is high) rate how much resistance you feel to each of these changes. Record your ratings.

(2) Are you expressing this resistance to others, or is it all inside you?

(3) Choose the change on your list you need most to say no to. If you could share with someone you trust the reasons why you resist this change, what would you say? Is there someone you want/need to share these reasons with?

2. Think of something you want very much to see changed and identify at least one person who is opposing this change.

(1) Try to put yourself in the person's place who is opposing the change. State as clearly as you can his/her reasons for opposing the change. Write them down.

(2) Which of the following techniques, if any, have you been using with the person who opposes the change? Which has been most effective? Which has been most ineffective? Why?
- Advice giving
- Listening
- Persuading
- Disagreeing
- Controlling
- Understanding
- Punishing

(3) In light of what you discovered in putting yourself in the other person's place, are there any new ways you can relate to this person which may be more helpful for him/her and for you?

6

Lord, give us wisdom
for removing fabricated barriers
which separate us from one another.
And replace them with joy
in sharing the human adventure.

—Billie Pate

6
Listening to Strangers

We learned it at an early age, "Don't talk to strangers!"
"Keep the door locked; don't let any strange person inside."

"Don't get in the car with anyone you don't know well."

Not bad advice because strangers are potentially threatening.

The threat of the stranger—the newcomer, the outsider, the "different one"—persists throughout our lives. People who are new, unknown, unusual, not of our own environment—different—get our attention. Persons unknown to us or different from us may turn out to be enemies or friends. They may bless our lives or curse us. They may help us or harm us. They may affirm us or confront us. They may even destroy us.

People who are different from us introduce change into our lives. In fact, the most powerful change forces in our lives are created by people different from us. They show us alternative ways of thinking, behaving, and believing. They make us question the current conditions of our lives.

Years ago I worked with a colleague who rubbed me the wrong way. We were very different. Here's the way I saw her: She was so concerned about details, she got lost in them. I was more often interested in "the big picture." She was precise in language and thought; so precise, in fact, *how* something was said was more important than *what* was said. By contrast, I was more concerned with the spirit of the matter—meaning rather than words. She wanted everything to be handled rationally, logically, dispassionately, and unemotionally. I appreciated reason and logic, but I believed some emotional expression was also appropriate since all of us have feelings as well as thoughts to deal with. She was thoroughly pragmatic. Starting with action, she judged things based primarily on whether they would work—*why* was a secondary, even unimportant question. I wanted to know as much of the *why* as I could.

At first I thought I could never adjust to a working relationship with this person. I wanted out. I liked my work, but continuing to do the work meant I was interdependent with her. I had to decide how to respond to her differences, how to manage the conflict I felt building with her.

Initially, I avoided her as much as I could. This was a technique to keep the conflict from escalating. Then I majored on finding her strong points and giving her credit in my mind where credit was due. Later I learned to tolerate her differences. Then I learned to respect and appreciate some of them. Eventually my own life was enriched—changed by some of her differences.

How can we open ourselves appropriately to persons who seem different from us? How can we listen to persons who are very different from us to understand them before we listen to judge them? How can we exhibit the Christian ideals of love of neighbor and brotherly love and live out of the biblical suggestion: "Don't forget to be kind to strangers, for some who have done this have entertained angels without realizing it" (Heb. 13:2, TLB). One translation of the latter part of this passage says, "for hereby have some entertained messengers" (Rotterham Emphasized New Testament). As difficult as it is, we are called on all our lives to listen to strangers—the different ones.

People Are Different

While each of us has some characteristics in common with all humankind, each of us is different—unique. Our differences may be slight and unnoticeable, or they may be so great as to make others strange to us.

People come in different sizes, shapes, and colors. We are different in age. We live in different cultures and subcultures. We live in different neighborhoods. We speak different languages. We have different amounts of formal education. We are diverse in our beliefs, attitudes, and values. We have different skills. Our life-styles are different. Our thought processes work differently. Difference. Difference. We bring our differences to our relationships with each other, and our differences repel or attract us to one another. Sometimes our differences make us strangers to each other and put us on our guard even with the people closest to us.

Our relationships and our differences become the raw material out of which we build life. Our differences help us create or destroy, grow or stagnate—change.

One person has a talent for writing poetry and another for composing music; they can link their differences to create a song.

One person takes action quickly and risks a lot, and another person moves more slowly and deliberately; their differences can complement each other, or they can harm each other by critizing the difference in the other.

One group of church members is more committed to mission action, and another group is more committed to evangelism. They can act out of their special commitments and support each other in helping create a balanced church program, or one group can try to require another group to change to its position with resulting conflict.

Relationships with persons who are different from us bring us a mixture of feelings—hope and despair, fulfillment and frustration, joy and sorrow.

The worlds in which we live out our relationships are increasingly different from what they once were. More and more differences are introduced into our experiences. Often the differences are dramatic. Each difference—large or small—confronts us with the possibility of change. Differences between us and others bring us face to face with strangers. Differences cause us to feel closer to or estranged from others.

Refugees settle in our neighborhood, and we are confronted with cultural influences completely different from our own.

A mother decides to work, and family routines are suddenly different.

Parents get old and are not as independent as they once were; they need a different kind of relationship with their children.

Differences—Creative or Destructive?

I once consulted with the principal and faculty of a private Catholic high school for girls. I was helping them manage some conflicts they were experiencing—conflicts, which grew out of differences and which made them strangers to each other.

The school had a history of high standards and effective results in secondary education. Graduation from the school all but guaranteed a young woman successful college entrance. Owned and operated by a congregation of Catholic nuns, the school's faculty and staff had largely been made up of nuns with a strong commitment to teaching. They were not only committed but also highly competent in what they did.

Then changes began to crowd in on the school. Over a period of time the nieghborhood in which the school was originally founded shifted dramatically from a higher income to a lower income population. The black population began to outnumber the white population. Transporting of students into the neighborhood, and the addition of neighborhood students broke up the cohesive patterns of extracurricular activities. A fierce school spirit was disturbed. Lay teachers were added to the faculty. Black teachers were added. Male teachers were added. The school enrollment shifted from all white students to a few black students, to a majority of black students.

The changes came bit by bit and piece by piece as the nuns tried to make their mission relevant to the needs around them. Alongside all the other changes, the financial base of the school eroded. The financial problems compounded all the other issues.

There were conflicts between students, between faculty and students, between faculty members, and between faculty members and parents. No one intended the conflict. In fact, all parties were surprised by it. No one was comfortable with the conflict. It caused feelings and behaviors which were not consistent with the Christian ideals of the persons involved.

The principal of the school was looking for help in dealing with massive changes and conflicts almost too complex to cope with. After preliminary work with the principal, I worked directly with the faculty—about twenty persons in all. I felt helping the principal and faculty came first because this might enable them in turn to help students and parents.

In my first meeting with the faculty, I used a visual model to help faculty members communicate with each other in as constructive a way as possible. I gave them the following instructions at a pace they could follow:

(1) Form a large circle. Think of the circle as a large wheel which is helping the school move along.

(2) Imagine spokes running from where you stand to a hub in the center of the wheel.

(3) Think of the hub as the decision-making center in the school where there is power to make the wheel move.

(4) Take a position on the wheel based on where you see yourself in your ability to influence what is happening in the school. Move beyond the edge of the wheel if you feel you do not have any vital decision-making influence in the school. Stay on the edge of the wheel if you feel you have a marginal influence on what is happening in the school. Move into the spoke and hub area if you feel you

have some influence on decision making in the school, with the strongest influence near the hub.

Each person took a position. Then I asked them to follow through on another set of instructions:

(1) Look around to see whether you feel comfortable with where other people have placed themselves.

(2) Move any person you feel should be in another position to a position which seems more appropriate.

They cast uncomfortable glances at each other. No one moved anybody else at first. Then a nun stepped toward a man standing at the outer edge of the wheel. Without a word, she extended her hand and pulled him halfway toward the hub. There was a sudden flurry of activity. People were being moved around like Chinese checkers— sometimes gently, sometimes with a nudge, or a slight push.

I stopped the action again and asked them to reflect on their experiences:

(1) Think about the original position you took plus the positions other people put you in. What do you think each of the positions meant?

(2) Take the position on the visual model (the wheel) which is now comfortable to you. Has your position changed?

(3) Sit on the floor and mark your position so we can talk about the picture we have just created.

Three nuns were near the hub. A Catholic priest, a male lay teacher, and a female lay teacher were completely outside the circle. Several lay teachers and one nun were on the edge of the circle. Several nuns and one lay teacher were in various positions on the spokes leading to the hub.

To the extent they were comfortable, I asked them to share answers to several questions; How do you feel about your position in the group? Can you explain the position you are in? How did you feel when someone moved you? Are you surprised about where anyone else in the group is?

People started talking. The information flow was moving at a fast pace. One of the lay teachers on the outside of the circle shook her head and said aloud, "I'm different!" No one heard her.

After a little while she said it in a louder voice, with some anger showing through, "I'm different!" Still no one acknowledged hearing her.

It happened a third time.

I pointed out to the group, "Margaret has said something to the group three times, and no one has acknowledged hearing her." Then, turning to Margaret I said, "Margaret, do you want to tell the group again what you said?"

Margaret shrugged her shoulders and told the group, "I'm different!" Then she added, "I'm black! I'm married! I'm Protestant!" (And I thought *how much more different can one get?* The group, most of whom were nuns, was primarily white, unmarried, and Catholic.)

The truth started coming out. Differences were not being handled creatively. One lay teacher said: "The school is your whole life [referring to a nun]. You don't mind how long after-school activities last because when you finish you walk across the yard to the convent where someone has prepared a meal for you. We have to go home and pick up our family responsibilities there and cook our own dinner. It is not as easy for us to stay long hours after school as it is for you."

Then a nun said, "Please don't stereotype all of us. We are all nuns, but we are different too. I'm different!"

I asked, "How many of you feel you are different?" The nods were affirmative. I suggested that we all say at one time, "I'm different! I'm different!"

I asked them to say it again and added "And it is OK to be different." "I'm different, and it is OK to be different."

"Say it one more time," I requested.

"I'm different, and it is OK to be different," they said in unison.

By now the group was beginning to celebrate its differences. We moved through a series of discussions to find ways to understand the differences and to blend them into the life of the school, making the differences creative rather than destructive. We made some progress.

People Need People

The episodes of conflict and discord in our relationships with others may be negative, but they affirm our interdependence with each other. They signal that we need each other. If we do not care about a person, differences do not matter much. We can avoid the person. If we do not need a relationship with a group of people, these people are not the focus of our attention. We can ignore them. But when we are interdependent with others in significant ways, we cannot avoid or ignore their differences. The differences confront us! They are part of a vital relationship—one we need, one we must depend on.

The truth is: *We tend only to get into conflict with persons who are important to us, persons with whom we are interdependent in some significant way.*

Persons who need one another the most are the most susceptible to conflict. Employers and employees need each other; they are interdependent. Teachers and students are essential to learning; one cannot get along without the other. Departments, divisions, and units are interdependent in an organization. As institutions, churches and schools are interdependent with the family; they need each other. Husbands and wives need each other as do parents and children.

The Bible contains beautiful imagery which describes interdependence in the body of Christ—the church. "The eye can never say to the hand, 'I don't need you.' . . . If one part suffers all parts suffer with it, and if one part is honored, all the parts are glad" (1 Cor.2:21,26, TLB).

It is not surprising, then, that some of our most severe conflicts come with people we care about most. Engaging others—even in conflict—indicates that these people are important to us and cannot be ignored.

We were created by God for relationship. Much of the quality of our lives is rooted in relationships essential to our well-being. When our significant relationships are good, life is good. When our relationships are poor, life is impoverished. Think back to some of the most painful times in your life. Didn't they come at a point where you experienced discord, distructive conflict, alienation, or loss in a relationship you depended on?

A pastor of a small church was at odds with the congregation over several issues. In a desperate effort to win the support of one group in the church, he supported the youth and young adults in their dream of building a recreation building (even when present church facilities were underused).

The pastor met with the younger group in private. They worked on a plan in which they called the proposed new building "educational." Then the pastor came to the congregation (with a large membership of elderly people) to have a "free and open discussion" about the proposal.

Intergenerational conflict erupted. The pastor had unwisely taken sides with younger members. The younger members had a dream and the energy and drive to work on it, but the older people had most of the resources and the bulk of the decision-making power. Battle ensued. The younger and older generations were estranged, alienated from each other.

In a business meeting, the older people made a motion to carpet the auditorium, to refinish the pews and to put padded cushions on them—and, when these projects were completed, to begin improving another part of the building. The motion passed. The next day a committee went out to select the carpet. What little building funds were available were now committed. The proposal from the young people was effectively blocked.

There was conflict between the old and the young.

Pain was intense. Underlying conflicts between church members and the pastor focused into severe conflict. Several people left the church. The pastor resigned.

How Conflict Develops

The example of conflict within a congregation illustrates that in severe conflict persons take rigid positions in opposition to one another's differences. In extreme conflicts, someone wins and someone loses on the *issues* involved. But everyone loses on *relationships*. Before conflict gets to this extreme phase, however, it always moves through several lesser phases. By recognizing these earlier and less severe phases, we may be able to deal with our conflicts while they are more manageable.

The phases we tend to go through in getting into conflict are outlined below and discussed later in the chapter.

Phase I: Becoming aware of differences in another person(s) and deciding how to respond; then testing the response. If the chosen response works, differences may be resolved adequately in this phase. In this case, conflict is minimal. If the response we choose does not work, Phase II occurs.

Phase II: Labeling the differences in another person(s) and reevaluating how to respond; then testing the response. More decision-making effort is expended at this phase and conflicts are either resolved or heightened. If they are not resolved, Phase II may be repeated again with a new label or the situation moves into Phase III.

Phase III: Taking a position in opposition to differences in another person(s). In this phase conflict is full blown, very intense, and difficult to manage.

Phases I and II involve making decisions about how to respond to differences in another person or group. Phase III is a decision to respond by opposing the differences in the other person(s).

Next we will take a look at what is involved as we become aware of differences, label differences, and take positions in opposition to differences.

Becoming Aware of Differences

The differences between us and others come to our attention more quickly when we are interdependent in some way—when we must depend on each other. At a department store, for instance, I become temporarily interdependent with the clerk. I need the clerk to handle my purchase. The clerk needs me to complete a sale. Even in brief moments of interdependence, we can experience differences which create conflict. I am in a hurry and want the clerk to focus on helping me as quickly as possible. The clerk is trying to give attention to several persons at the same time and is delaying the completion of my transaction. I feel impatient and frustrated.

If conflicts can so easily develop with nameless strangers, how much more are conflicts likely to be present with persons close to us. The persons closest to us have the most potential to rub us the wrong way. Husbands and wives, parents and children, employees and employers, committee members, friends, neighbors, church staff members—the list is almost endless. In the intimate, close relationships of life we are face-to-face with vast differences.

You think intuitively.	I think logically.
I enjoy classical music.	You enjoy country western music.
You value structured activity.	I value spontaneity.
I like to get jobs done ahead of time, without pressure.	You procrastinate doing tasks because you are energized by pressure.
I like to work with a democratic leader.	You are an authoritarian leader.
I believe the Bible is literally true.	You don't.
You are older with power to get things done,	I am young and full of raw energy but I don't

but you are low on energy.

I am messy.

You are careful and cautious.

I squeeze my toothpaste from the bottom of the tube, rolling the tube carefully as it empties.

I can walk.

have the decision-making clout to get things done.

You are neat.

I am adventurous and risking.

You squeeze the toothpaste tube any where you can grab it.

You cannot use your legs and ride in a wheelchair.

As we relate to other persons, we are constantly weighing differences—consciously or unconsciously. When we spot a difference, we evaluate what it means to us. We feel comfortable or uncomfortable about it. If we feel the least bit uncomfortable, we listen to the person's words and watch the person's actions to prove or disprove our early impressions. We decide how to respond. Then we start testing to determine whether our early impressions are true. We may revise our impressions. But, if the impression seems true, we decide how to respond to the difference. If we are the least bit uncomfortable, we may label the difference.

Labeling Differences

Labels are ways we describe, classify, or designate differences. They are shortcuts to communication. Say "boss" and everyone understands. Say "drug addict" and the designation is clear. The picture is in place quickly when we call someone a "hawk" or a "dove." "Snob" is unambiguous.

While labels serve useful purposes in providing shortcuts to communication, they also are dangerous.

"Tom is autocratic."

"Betty is a liberal."

Labels depersonalize persons and reduce them to

categories. Labels round off the edges of individuality and stuff persons into pigeon holes. Labels become stereotypes which communicate fixed, unvarying ideas about people, groups, events, or issues. When used to describe persons, stereotypes are oversimplified conceptions or opinions or beliefs about that person.

Think how commonly we use stereotypic labels. Here are only a few: conservative, spendthrift, troublemaker, red-neck, autocrat, liberal, good ol' boy, smart aleck.

If we have trouble dealing with a person—if the person is threatening to us in some way—we can put the person in a category. If we can get the person labeled, we can relate in the way we know how to relate to people with that label. If I can call you a red-neck, I don't have to deal with the validity of your political or racial views.

As you and I label others, we no longer have to deal with them as persons; we can deal with them as a type or a category. Labeling is a part of our defense against the "stranger" part of that person—the difference which bothers us and which might change us.

Response to Differences

We have several options for responding to differences in other persons. We may deny that differences are even present, ignore them, tolerate them, accept them, or reject them.

A friend with a twisted hand missing a thumb and two fingers told me she is aware of how people respond to her hand which is different. Some people act as if it doesn't exist; they deny or ignore it. Others are so aware of the hand they can hardly take their eyes off it in a kind of morbid tolerance. Some people accept it for what it is— neither denying nor ignoring it.

A deformed hand is one thing. Other kinds of differences are something else. A deformed hand is not "catching." But a lot of the differences we encounter in other people can be caught. They can change us.

Different beliefs, attitudes, values, behaviors, and

skills can be learned from other persons. If we accept the differences in another person, we may come to respect the difference, value it, learn from it, and become different too. *The possibility of being changed by another person's difference is the ultimate threat.* Saying no to the difference is our way of saying no to change. The rejection of the difference is our defense against change.

When we reject differences in other persons, we usually move to dislike the differences, devalue them, refuse to learn from them, and defend ourselves against being changed by them. A part of our defense is to build a stronger case for our own position and against the other. Our position becomes emotionally invested. We feel stronger about it. We talk more loudly and intensely about it. We move toward a rigid stand which declares "I am right" and "he is wrong," or "we are right" and they are wrong," or "I am normal" and "she is abnormal."

How Conflict Builds

The following experience from the life of a teacher illustrates how conflict builds.

A high school teacher notices students who have long hair and a generally unkempt appearance. The teacher becomes aware of the difference and begins to think about what it means. *Is this an effort on the part of students to express their individuality? Does this represent slippage in standards of personal appearance in the school? Does this signal disorder in the school, a rejection of authority?* The teacher evaluates how important the difference is.

If the difference is judged to be unimportant or inconsequential, it does not become an issue. The difference is tolerated or accepted. But, if the difference poses a threat, the teacher will begin to use words or phrases to label the difference. The teacher calls the students "dirty" or "troublemakers" or labels them "disrespectful." The label may be libel, but the teacher labels the difference.

Labeling of differences usually stereotypes the person who is different rather than identifying the real concern of the labelers. And when this happens, some of the more basic issues get lost. The label begins to reduce the person to a type. Personal identity gets lost in a category. The person is no longer dealt with as a person but as a type of person. Characteristics ascribed to the "type of person" are assigned along with the label.

This phase is a crucial one. Conflict now builds very rapidly. Persons who are different become "the enemy." Depersonalization increases. Persons are referred to by the impersonal pronouns "they" and "them." Personal names are used less and less. Relationships become more and more strained. Imperceptibly, the conflict may sweep into Phase III. The teacher declares, "We must get rid of long hair and dirty clothes." The teacher takes a firm position in opposition to the difference.

When one person takes a firm stand, the other person usually responds with a firm stand. The position of each gets set in concrete. From this point on, the battle rages. Each person fights to win. And, in order for one to win, the other must lose. A win-lose battle ensues. Someone does win. However, as one of my friends used to say, "He won, but he didn't get nothin'." The victory is a hollow victory. Relationships have been damaged in the process—relationships between persons who are interdependent with each other in some significant way.

But back to Phase II. Once labeling begins to occur, another sequence of events is possible. If persons begin to feel uncomfortable with what is happening, they may back off and reevaluate the differences and how they are responding to them. The teacher, for example, may begin to question why the differences became such a big issue. The teacher may try to keep the relationship with the student personalized. The teacher may decide that keeping a relationship with the student is more important than the difference involved. The teacher may even let the student know he is bothered by his appearance but communicate to the student that he doesn't want it to interfere with the teaching-learning process any more than it has to. The teacher reevaluates the difference and decides how to respond—the difference is tolerated or accepted.

Deciding How to Respond

When we begin to feel the pangs of conflict with another person or group, we can ask ourselves some questions to think through how we are feeling and responding. These questions help us apply our minds to the issues as well as our emotions. Thinking systematically about what we are feeling often helps us control and direct our emotional responses. Talking aloud with a trusted friend or counselor also helps. Here are a few questions which are usually helpful:

1. *Do I believe the other person has a right to be different?* This question calls us back to the fact that people are different in ways they can and can't control. In the providence of God, each person is unique with individual capacity for freedom, choice, and responsibility. Each person, once he reaches maturity, not only has a right but also a responsibility to choose his course of action.

While there are limits on freedom, of course, each person has a right to it. And that right should not be abridged lightly. Whether I agree or not, another person has a right to different choices about his beliefs, attitudes, values, and behaviors. If another person and I are committed to each other in a relationship, however, I do have the right to call that person to accept the responsible limits on freedom which our relationship entails. But, granting others their right to be different establishes their worth and value in the midst of whatever differences exist.

2. *What difference in the other person is bothering me?* Be specific. Is it something the person believes? Is it an attitude? Is it something the person values? Is it appearance? Is it behavior—something the person does? Keep probing. Usually we can discover some behaviors— some ways a person acts; something a person does. Focusing very specifically on the difference which is bothering us keeps us from blanketing the whole relation-

ship with problems. The first step in solving any problem is to identify it clearly. And this is the most difficult step.

3. *What do I fear most about the difference in the other person?* What is the worst thing that could happen because of the difference? The ultimate threat is that you and I will be changed in ways we don't want, or even be destroyed by the difference in the other person. Looking straight at our fears helps us see whether they are as big or bigger than we thought, whether they are smaller or larger proportionately than they need to be. Facing our fears helps us decide whether the fear is reasonable or unreasonable, wise or absurd. At times we can give up a fear after evaluating it. At other times we must honor our fears and live with them as we appropriately protect ourselves and/or others.

4. *Do I understand the difference from the other person's point of view?* When we are threatened, we tend to defend. When another person's difference rubs us the wrong way, we tend to see our own difference as the better one. We start listening to judge the other person rather than listening to understand. Communication with the other person becomes very difficult.

The only way to break down the barriers—if we want to—is to open ourselves to the other person. When we listen to understand, we are often surprised by what we learned. When we jog in another person's Nikes, things may not look the same at all. A superficial judgment on our part may be confirmed or disconfirmed. But until we pay the price to understand another we cannot know.

Understanding comes through communication which is two-way—listening as well as speaking, understanding as well as hearing, feeling with as well as feeling about.

Genuine communication may result in agreement or disagreement about the issues involved in the relationship, but—even in disagreement—the other person is accepted as a person of worth and value. Even when tough issues of disagreement must be dealt with, these are dealt with on a base of respect, love, and appropriate trust.

The ideal of this quality of relationship is difficult to comprehend in purely human terms. We have to learn from our relationship with God who respects, loves, and trusts us. We have to imitate Christ, the compassionate one. And we have to rely on the Spirit of God dwelling within us to awaken our best capacities as persons created in God's image.

5. *How do I choose to respond to the difference in another person*. Accent the word *choose*. We do choose. Contrary to what we think, we have the capacity to choose to deny, ignore, tolerate, accept, or reject differences in other people.

To accept responsibility for the choice we make in responding to another person's difference is both a burden and a joy. The passage in Matthew 5:39 which says, "If you are slapped on one cheek, turn the other too" (TLB) may mean that the Christian way is staying in control of our actions and choosing deliberately how to respond. A slap on the cheek can trigger the automatic response of slapping back. We react defensively! At least one significant part of the Christian message may be that God made us capable of choosing—even under the most difficult of circumstances—how we will respond. It *is* possible to turn the cheek rather than give in to the natural tendency of slapping back.

Is there hope, then, that we can choose to listen to strangers—the different ones? There are some benefits which come to those who listen and understand across the barriers of difference.

We can come to appreciate differences between us and others which enrich our lives. If we were all alike, the world would be a dull place. We can learn consciously to appreciate and affirm differences as part of God's creative design.

We can appreciate and affirm the way in which we and others are alike. We hold in common with other people the same basic needs—to feel secure, to belong, to be appreciated, to be valued for our uniqueness, to be loved, to have expression for our unique gifts, to fulfill our God-given possibilities. We all need relationships with God and with each other.

By respecting differences, we can deliberately choose how to respond to the differences that threaten to destroy us or our families, our churches, our schools, our work settings. We can challenge these differences—even change them—without destroying our relationships with significant other persons who are important and essential to us.

In handling differences creatively, we manage our conflict and discover new levels of joy in sharing the human adventure with others.

Managing Conflict

Managing conflict does not always mean eliminating differences or even resolving them. *The goal of conflict management is to help us deal creatively rather than destructively with our differences.* Management of conflict implies that conflict can be a positive force to be controlled and directed, handled and used. Positive outcomes in conflict have to be sought; they rarely automatically happen.

Conflict can be positive and creative. Conflict gets the adrenalin flowing. People in conflict are energized, excited, talkative, engaged, and animated. Issues and unresolved questions are lifted to the surface and dealt with. Creative tension, friendly competition, mediation, and reconciliation are possible in the midst of conflict. The most challenging possibility of all is that the best differences of persons will get integrated into an improved condition for the persons involved in the conflict.

The negative outcome in conflict is always a possibility however. As conflict builds, destructive forces come into play very quickly. As one person or group takes a firm stand in opposition to another person or group, each becomes more and more convinced the other is wrong. Strong, almost overpowering forces begin to operate. Ideas and opinions of people clash. People express anger and hostility toward one another. The emotional climate becomes so intense each person or group feels compelled to fight or take flight from the conflict. Each person, in effect, reevaluates one more time how to respond to the difference between himself and another or between his group and another group. If a decision is made to oppose the position of the other, each person struggles to win. A win-lose battle ensues.

The need to win drives persons to focus on another person or group as "the enemy" and to attack in every way possible. The enemy is listened to not to be understood but to probe his weak points and to locate his position for another round of battle.

Labeling and name-calling increase. Motives of all parties become suspect. Persons increasingly depersonalize each other. Communication becomes more and more distorted. People lose their feelings of warmth and caring for each other. Relationships become cold and distant. Experiencing great pain and discomfort, people on each side of the conflict come to believe being right is worth that price.

In the most extreme conflict, physical violence occurs, and the enemy is literally destroyed. More often, in one form or another, someone wins and someone loses. Winning occurs through a majority vote, a legal opinion, a resignation, or forcing the other person to give in.

Finding Help

When we are involved in conflict, we need to find help to make the outcomes positive rather than negative. This help may be help we give ourselves, help we receive from God, or help which comes from other persons. Persons who are skilled in recognizing and dealing with conflict can help themselves and others in a conflict situation. It is easier to help others, however, than to help oneself. When we are a part of a conflict, we are likely to become so subjectively involved in it that all of our good skills do not or cannot come into play.

116

The first step in helping manage a conflict is to determine where we are in relationship to it. If you or I are one of the parties to the conflict, we can expect to have trouble getting and keeping our perspective. We will have trouble looking at issues objectively. This probably is one reason Ann Landers gets so many letters about fighting among in-laws! But the fact remains: A person who is skilled in managing conflict can help himself, as well as help others, though self-help is more difficult.

When we are involved in conflicts which are ongoing and intense, self-help is less and less an option. Help from a more neutral person becomes almost essential. A neutral person is someone who is not directly involved in the conflict, someone who has some skills for dealing with conflict, and someone acceptable to parties in conflict.

Some persons because of their positions in an organization, in the family, or professionally are in helping roles. A principal, for instance, can be a neutral helper in conflict between students and a teacher or between parents and a teacher. A supervisor can help two employees manage their differences. A minister can help individuals and groups within the church membership deal with their differences. A parent is in a position to help children settle their disputes. A counselor is trained specifically in helping skills.

Whether we help ourselves or seek help from someone else in a conflict situation, we need to stay sensitive to the level or intensity of the conflict. Sometimes tension levels are not high enough for both parties in conflict to deal with the issues. In this case, a helping person has to wait for or help tensions escalate to a higher level so people are more ready to deal with the issues. Solomon did this in settling the conflict between two women who were in dispute over ownership of a baby. Only when Solomon threatened to divide the baby in half did the tension level get sufficiently high for the issue to be dealt with.

A helping person sometimes has to provide a safe environment for people to ventilate their strong feelings so tensions which have become too high can be reduced to productive levels.

Being the Helper in Conflict

In helping others deal with conflict, there are a few techniques which—when used with skill—usually produce positive results. A few of these are listed here.

1. *Help persons appreciate their differences and their needs for each other.* Suggest that personal and group differences are an asset as well as a liability in relationships. When persons are caught in conflict, they tend to see it only as bad or undesirable. They need to be helped to understand that their conflict signals that they are important to each other. Each cares enough to engage rather than to ignore the other person. They need each other. The relationship is important to both. Helping persons get this perspective often helps them relax enough to deal with the conflict.

2. *Help persons clarify their differences.* Sometimes the real issues get lost. The issues have to be refocused. The basic questions persons need to keep answering with greater and greater clarity are: What are we in conflict about? Are we in conflict about all parts or some parts of the issue? Why are our differences so important? What are the most destructive outcomes that could happen out of our conflict? Are we willing to risk having these happen? If not, what are some of the steps we can take to deal with our differences in constructive ways? Clarification of issues or problems is a big first step toward resolution.

3. *Help persons deal with each other as persons.* Persons need to be called on to deal with each other as real persons and not as stereotypes or as "the enemy." Face-to-face contact helps do this. Persons in conflict need to be encouraged to call each other by their given names rather than "he," "she," "they," and "the boss." Persons need to be encouraged to look at each other as they speak because the personhood of another cannot be ignored when we look into that person's eyes. A helper can encour-

age persons to stay in personal contact, look at each other, and call each other by name.

4. *Help persons hear and be heard by each other.* Communication becomes exceedingly difficult between/ among persons in conflict. Words filter through intense emotions and become emotionally charged. People have trouble listening to one another, let alone understanding. People begin to listen selectively to hear what they want to hear. Powerful negative nonverbal signals are exchanged—looks of anger, avoidance of eye contact, avoidance of any contact. A helper can aid communication by encouraging persons to clarify their messages to each other, by helping persons listen first to understand rather than to judge, and by helping persons keep two-way communication going.

5. *Save persons from the pressure of premature decision making.* Nothing escalates conflict more than the pressure of an impending decision. Decisions force issues very quickly—sometimes too quickly. Pacing and time become crucial factors in conflict management. People are helped when decisions are paced so there are periods of information gathering and discussion before the formal act of decision making. People are often helped when they have time to test something in an experimental form before they are aked to commit to it more substantially.

Conflict too often means that someone loses and someone wins. Some persons live predominantly out of this assumption. Competition is the game, and gamesmanship is the skill!

Some of the great rewards in life go to persons who can help control and direct potential conflict to a constructive end. Occasionally, when the stakes are high enough because of values or principles, a person or group must try to win at almost any cost. But the all-or-nothing situation may not be required as often as we sometimes think.

> Lord,
> I know I can trust the promise—

Love will deal with hate,
Caring will overcome indifference,
Sharing will beat selfishness,
Peace will win over war,
Brotherhood will put down prejudice,
and joy will leave no cause for crying.
Lord,
together, we can make the promise so.

Billie Pate

For Your Reflection

1. Make a list of the persons with whom you are most interdependent, persons on whom you depend and who depend on you. By each person's name, indicate his or her relationship to you—spouse, child, friend, employer. Think about your relationship with each person.

    (1) Have you ever experienced conflict with any of these persons?

    (2) How much or how little do you agree with this statement; We tend only to get into conflict with persons who are important to us, persons with whom we are interdependent in some significant way.

2. Choose one person from your list. List all the ways you can think of that you and that person are different. Label one column I am, believe, feel, can, think, etc. Label the other column he/she is, believes, feels, thinks, etc.

    (1) Put a plus (+) by the differences on your list which make each of you better and stronger because the difference exists.

    (2) Put a minus (—) by the differences on your list which irritate the two of you the most and which cause conflict between you.

    (3) Go through each difference again and code it A, B, C, or D according to the way you most typically respond to it (the specific differences, not the person):

A. Ignore it
B. Tolerate it
C. Accept it
D. Reject it
Look at your codes alongside your pluses and minuses. Do you see any relation between the two? Are the items you put a plus by coded *C* more often, for example?

3. Identify another person on the list you made in step 1 with whom you currently feel some conflict because of your differences. Answer these questions:

(1) Do I believe (name the other person) has a right to be different?

(2) What differences in (name the other person) are bothering me?

(3) What do I fear most about the difference between (name the other person) and me?

(4) Do I understand the difference from (name the person) point of view?

(5) How do I choose to respond to this difference?

4. Which of these statements best describes you?

___ I always try to avoid conflict because it makes me very uncomfortable.

___ I do not mind conflict if it is not too intense—conflict can be lively, energizing, and creative.

___ I usually am drawn toward conflict—I enjoy a good fight.

If the statement you checked is the best one of the three to describe you but it still does not fit, write a statement which does describe you.

5. Think of one of the worst conflict situations you remember experiencing (in your past, not in your present). This conflict might have been between you and another person or between two groups of people. Use this experience as a case study. Answer these questions:

(1) What persons or groups of persons were on opposing sides?

(2) What were the real issues between persons or

groups who were in opposition to each other?

(3) Did the original issue which precipitated the conflict hold throughout the conflict, or did the conflict shift to other issues? Did differences get more sharply focused or did they get broader and more inclusive as the conflict moved along?

(4) Which of these characteristics do you remember observing?

__ a commitment to win on both sides which meant the other side had to lose

__ making the opposing person or group "the enemy"

__ planning ways to attack "the enemy" at his weakest point

__ depersonalizing the opposition, speaking of "they," "them" rather than calling names

__ questioning the real motives of the opposition

__ difficulty in achieving clear communication between the two opposing persons/groups

__ each group hearing what was said only to build a strategy against the other rather than understand the other

__ cold and distant feelings toward the opposition

__ exchanging of loud talk and strong nonverbal signals—looks of anger, avoidance of eye contact, moving away from

__ violent, destructive behavior

__ winning by majority vote, legal opinion, resignation, or giving in

__ losing

(5) If you could be a neutral helper in that conflict situation now, what specific things would you do to help the people involved?

6. Think of a current conflict situation in which you could be a neutral helper. How can you help?

7

The road to realizing my dreams
Seems to grow steadily steeper.
Could it be
At one of those turns on the way
I left behind
My purpose for living
My willingness to reach out
to help and be helped?

—Billie Pate

7

Reducing the Costs of Change

Mother sent me to the store to buy some hamburger. In our small town, the store was not far away. As a seven-year-old, I invited one of my friends to go along. Doris Jean and I talked about how much we wished we each had a penny to put in the bright red candy ball machine in front of Anna Miller's Variety Store.

Then I had a brilliant idea—or so it seemed at the time. I got two buttons about the size of pennies from my mother's sewing box. "We will use these," I told Doris Jean. I felt proud of the way I had solved the no-pennies problem.

The buttons were the right diameter but they were too thick to go into the machine. This new problem called for another creative solution. "We can rub the buttons on the sidewalk and make them thinner," I suggested. Doris Jean and I started rubbing, then trying them in the machine for size, then rubbing again. Making the buttons thinner was a slow process.

Anna Miller appeared in the store doorway and inquired about what we were doing. We quickly hid the buttons in our hands—hot from the friction of rubbing on the sidewalk—and escaped her watchful eye by walking rapidly down the street toward the grocery store.

It was only then it occurred to me to feel guilty. I was suddenly conflicted deep inside myself. My heart ached and I felt the chill of fear creep over me. I wondered how I could ever go in Anna Miller's store again and look her in the face. And, *oh, what will happen when mother finds out?* I thought.

The original purpose for going to town got lost in the candy machine escapade. By the time Doris Jean and I went into the grocery store and returned home with the hamburger, we were long overdue. Mother's eyes were filled with question marks. Her voice was stern and demanding. "Where have you been all this time?" She was worried about us. Reluctantly I told the truth mostly because I was afraid Anna Miller would tell her if I didn't. Mother gave me a reprimand and a spanking. She also talked with me and hugged me.

That day I decided pretty theft was not worth the cost.

We are all cost conscious. When we try to satisfy our wants and needs, the how-much-does-it-cost question gets out early. We know there are limits on what we can afford to spend. If the costs are too high, we decide a particular want or need cannot be met or we shop around for a better price — one we can afford.

All change costs something. When we can calculate costs in dollars and cents or in days, hours, and minutes, we understand the costs better. Unfortunately some of the highest costs in making change are not that clear. They are the obscure hidden costs which we pay with a calorie of energy here and an emotional expenditure there. Change requires withdrawals from our limited resources of money, time, physical energy, and emotional strength.

If we perceive the cost of any change to be too high, we resist changing as long as we can. If we believe the benefits of a change are worth the cost, we open ourselves to it. If we are unsure, we decide how much or how little we are willing to risk changing.

Hidden Costs

The hidden costs of change are the personal private ones. When groups of people are involved in change projects they tend to assess costs in money and time. These kinds of costs are more easily calculated. We can estimate how much it will cost and how long it will take to replace an old house with a new one. We can determine the point in time and the cost of additional insurance for a teenager to be changed from a nondriver into a driver of a family automobile. We can establish dates for implementation, and we can assess the dollar costs of busing school children to achieve integration as a social change. We can mark in time the tragic loss of life to accident or illness. We can date the devastating disaster of a tornado, flood, earthquake, fire, or volcano and estimate the financial loss. But with each of the above changes, there are intensely personal and private costs to be paid by individuals. These are the high costs of such things as fear, grief, anxiety, tension, despair, stress, alienation, conflict, and hostility.

This book has already referred to the problems we have with our fears of the unknown, with our anxiety about the future, and with the alienation we experience when there is conflict between us and others. These kinds of problems exact their price. Other examples of some of the high costs of change are grief, tension, and stress.

1. *Grief.* One of the higher costs of change is grief. Sometimes it is a hidden cost. By the time we reach adulthood, most of the changes in our lives are "add ons." Change means something old has to be given up wholly or partially for something new. Loss and gain are both present. Loss means the complete absence or separation from a valued person or object. We know to expect big-scale losses, such as the loss of someone through death, to produce grief. But we do not know to expect grief in milder terms when we lose or are separated even temporarily from anyone or anything of significance to us.

In times of loss or separation, we move through a grief process to a new life adjustment, or we get lost in an incomplete process and fail at adjustment. The grief process may take a short time or a long time. Grief truly has its price.

Sometimes our grief is anticipatory. We know ahead of time that loss or separation is coming, and we have some time to prepare for it. This anticipation triggers a grief process which moves through the steps of denial, anger, bargaining, despair, and acceptance.

Sometimes loss comes suddenly and without warning. Grief is acute. In these cases, we experience shock, panic, and numbness. These feelings have to be dealt with first before we can work our way through the rest of the grief process. Grief is one of the higher costs of change.

2. *Tension.* In addition to grief, tension is another hidden cost of change. The cost may be too much or too little tension in life. In chapter 2, we talked about forces for and against change, forces which are in tension with each other. These tensions are real in individuals and in groups. Do-it-now *versus* do-it-later. No *versus* yes. Should I *versus* can I? Better *versus* best. Mistrust *versus* trust. Anxiety *versus* faith. Good *versus* evil. Immaturity *versus* maturity. Stability *versus* change. At the decision points of life, moderate amounts of tension are essential and healthy.

Tension can be illustrated with a rubber band. Put too much tension on it and it pops. Put too little or no tension on it and it simply doesn't do the things a rubber band is meant to do. Put moderate tension on it, and it does its job of holding things together.

Our lives are like the rubber band. When there is little or no tension in our lives, we pay a price. We become inert. We settle into dependable, comfortable routines. We live out of habit, without thinking. We experience apathy and indifference. There is no sense of urgency, no sense of necessity to deal with life's options. It is easy for us to ignore information which threatens us. Growth stops.

When there is too much tension in our lives, we pay a high price for it. Our capacity to stretch to assimilate new information is spent. We close out new options. We defend the status quo. We are immobilized. We stop growing and start defending. We are stretched to the limits. We run the risk of breakdown physically or emotionally.

When tension levels are moderate—neither too high nor too low—we grow and mature. We are aware of and relating to God and other people. We are questioning, searching, and integrating new information. We are enjoying, risking, testing, creating. We are changing.

For the sake of ourselves and others, we need to be aware of tension levels in order to keep them at moderate, productive levels—sometimes creating tension, sometimes escalating tension, and sometimes reducing tension. It takes all three.

3. *Stress.* Another hidden cost in change is stress. Stress is a generalized response to disturbances in our equilibrium. When we experience a high level of stress, we tend to perceive ourselves as being out of control. The conditions of our lives seem to be pressuring us from sources we cannot fully understnad. Life is out of balance.

Stress can be caused by events such as the birth of a child, a new job, requirements to work longer hours, illness, and increase in pace or amount of work activity. Stress also is caused by ongoing conditions in our lives, such as unresolved conflicts with other people, unclear roles and responsibilities, too much work to do in too little time, feedback only when performance is unsatisfactory, inadequate finances, pollution, noise, and anxiety about children.

I heard Wayne Oates, noted pastoral counselor, say that a lot of stress comes from the "mands" in our lives—demands, reprimands, commands, and remands. He tied a lot of our stress to expectations too: expectations of me by others, expectations of others by me, and expectations of myself by me.[1]

When the "mands" and expectations of life are reasonable, we can cope more easily. Unreasonable "mands" and expectations ignore our limits, calling on us to respond in ways we are not equipped to respond. Unreasonable expectations lead others or us to ignore limits beyond which we are equipped to go—individually or collectively.

When our limits are exceeded—for whatever reason—we strain to respond. The strains are both physical and emotional. The signs of strains are such things as hypertension, illness, insomnia, irritability, depression, negative attitudes, cynicism, quickness to anger, and chronic fatigue. Prolonged periods of unremitting stress can create a condition called burnout—exhaustion accompanied by a sense of futility.

Each of us has a responsibility to control the cost of change for ourselves and to help control the cost for others. We cannot do this alone, although a part of it we must do for ourselves. This is the paradoxical message in Paul's letter to the churches of Galatia. Paul wrote, "Carry each other's burdens and so live out the law of Christ" (Gal. 6:2, Phillips). But Paul also wrote "For every man must 'shoulder his own pack' " (Gal. 6:5, Phillips).

We work at cost control most effectively when we do it in the context of our relationships with God and with other people. We do it best when we plan and when we feel the support of caring persons.

Planning to Change

One of the most effective cost-cutting measures in change is planning. Planning causes us to decide what commitments we are willing to make and gives us a sense of direction and purpose.

1. *Purpose.* Life revolves around purpose, and planning starts with purpose. Purpose is our reason for being—the "why" of our existence. If the purpose of life or any part of life is not clear to us, we are in trouble.

Purpose characterizes organizations as well as individuals. A business organization might say its purpose is "to provide products and services at a profit." Your church might say its purpose is "to be a fellowship of baptized believers in Jesus Christ, experiencing the love and discipleship of God, loving and sharing a common life with one another, and seeking to bring all persons into the same relationship."

What purpose would you state for yourself in life? What purpose would you state for your family? For the person who has experienced salvation in Christ, the most basic call to purpose in life is the call to discipleship—the call to be a follower of Christ. This purpose is personal for each of us. Additionally we share common purposes with others to whom we are related—in our family, church, organizations, government.

Purpose dispels meaninglessness, giving meaning to what we do. We cannot possibly underestimate the devastating results which come when we have no sense of purpose, an unclear purpose, or a lost sense of purpose. In the absence of clear purpose—reason for living—life is lived in a vacuum which can so easily be filled with pessimism, cynicism, and despair. Activities become pointless; motion goes nowhere. A young mother, for example, can get lost in diapers and dishes and dissatisfaction when she loses sight of the purpose of child rearing. But when we live our lives with meaning and purpose—especially the meaning and purpose which God intends for us—we tap the sources of abundant life. Joy. Peace. Faith. Hope. Love.

Purpose is a stabilizer in life. It is so basic it is relatively unchanging. When a clear sense of purpose is present, this purpose becomes a dependable base for dealing with changing goals and plans. Purpose has an enduring quality. It provides stability in life. Paul expressed his commitment to purpose as follows: "One thing I do, forgetting what lies behind and straining forward to what lies ahead, I press on toward the . . . prize of the upward call of God in Christ Jesus" (Phil. 3:13-14, RSV).

2. *Goal Setting.* Goals are specific things we intend to happen tomorrow, next week, next month, or next year. We may write them down or carry them around in our heads, but our goals are specific things we expect to happen at specific points in time. They are so specific we can measure whether we attain them.

Goals are also statements of faith about our future.

For example, a couple concerned about being effective parents sets some goals such as "spend time as a family each Saturday for the next four weeks visiting historical points of interest in our community" or "start a family prayer time at breakfast each morning" or "make a family TV viewing schedule for the next month." Implementing these goals will not guarantee that the parents are more effective parents. But the goals do express commitment to the task of being parents, and they do express some first steps which might be taken to become better parents. The steps, then, are taken in the faith that they will produce results. As the first steps are taken, we discover other steps to take. "A man's mind plans his way but the Lord directs his steps" (Prov. 16:9, RSV).

Goals help us firm up our commitments and act on them. As a counselor for a Billy Graham crusade in Oklahoma City several years ago, I was impressed with the sensitivity of the persons who worked with Billy Graham. They understood the needs of persons to make decisions and commitments—to set goals. Persons making decisions for Christ were encouraged to identify specific things (goals) they would do in the next few weeks—reading and memorizing Scripture verses, establishing prayer as a daily activity, joining a church. These tangible goals helped persons firm up their commitments to God. This is the purpose of goals—to help us express our commitment to purpose in tangible concrete form—to help us change in constructive ways in line with worthy purposes.

Goals are made not only to be achieved but also to be changed. When we set goals, we are deciding on the best course of action we know to be available to us, based on whatever information we have to use at that time. More information, or better information received later, may cause us to change our plans. Changing plans based on improved information is an adjustment for the better. As a rule, the original goal and the changed one will both take us firmly in the direction of worthy purpose to be achieved.

Goals do not eliminate the risk taking of change, but they do allow us to calculate the risks. When we change through drifting or by accident, we have little opportunity to deal with risks and costs. They get beyond our control. The costs are paid before we are able to calculate them. But when we plan our change, when we decide our next steps, we are in a position to weigh the risks of change and the costs of changing.

3. *Past, Present, and Future.* Each of us has a past, a present, and a future. Each of these time frames is an important part of life—has been, is, and can be. The only shapable part of life, however, is the present. Some things can only be done in present moments, such as loving, caring, working. We do them now or the present moments are gone forever.

Sometimes we lose our present moments to our past or to our future. We deal with our past through our memories, and we deal with our future through vision. Both memory of the past and vision of the future are important to us. But spending excessive time with our memories or with our vision causes us to live in the past or the future rather than in the present.

Our past which we hold in memory has valuable information for living more effectively in the present. But our memories can also keep us from making the most of the present moments in life.

If our memories of the past are exceptionally pleasant, we might find it easier to live with our memories of the past rather than living today. A widowed spouse, for instance, sometimes lives in the past in the denial phase of grief during which memory of life and denial of death are sustaining forces.

If our memories of the past are unpleasant, we may be locked into guilt and shame about our past. These feelings cause us to spend more energy on our past than on our present. God's ancedote for guilt and shame is forgiveness. Forgiveness frees us from our past to take advantage of our present.

Our vision of the future can also rob us of our present. Thinking of an unknown future can create great anxiety, uncertainty, worry, and fear. Today can be lost worrying about tomorrow. God's ancedote for anxiety is trust and hope.

Planning allows us to stand right in the middle of the present and find the next steps to take today and tomorrow. In planning, we use our memory to recall experiences of yesterday and to draw from those experiences the information which will help us live today and tomorrow. In planning, we use our vision of the future—its possibilities and its problems—to decide what shape we desire our future to take. We make commitments to what we want to conserve and what we want to change. Then, in the present, we act in light of our future *and* our past. Rather than letting our past or our future cheat from us today, we call on our past and future to support us in the present moments of life. Doing this reduces the cost of change.

When action in the present is supported by information from the past and a plan for the future, we find life easier. Recently I overheard two men talking. One reported his window air-conditioning unit had "gone out." The fan quit working. He had to do something—change the fan or change the whole unit. In the course of talking, the man gave some information from the past—"the air conditioner is fifteen years old." He also gave some information about a future plan. He said, "Next year we plan to install central air-conditioning." Then I heard him report how he planned to solve his problem. "I decided to change to central air-conditioning now rather than spend the money making repairs or on replacing the window unit." This man's decision regarding present action was supported by information from the past and a plan for the future.

Plans for the future help us solve today's problems in light of tomorrow's hopes. Random solution of problems without a firm sense of future direction is wasteful and costly.

Planning is one of the most cost-effective ways to

work with change. Planning saves us from random choice, making change more purposive and intentional. Commitment to worthy purposes in life which are relatively stable, enduring, and unchangeing gives us the basis for choosing and making changes toward fulfillment of these purposes.

Support for Changing

Albert Schweitzer is credited with saying, "All of us live by what others have given us, often unwittingly, in the significant hours of our lives." Using this quote as a reference, I have sometimes written persons thanking them for special gifts they have given me at very significant moments in my life. I know I literally live by the trust, respect, loyalty, encouragement, and love people have given me through the years. My life is enriched by the advice, suggestions, reprimands, questions, and proddings from people who have my best interest at heart—and even from some people who do not.

Other people introduce change possibilities into our lives—alternative ways of thinking, feeling, believing, doing. Other people also give us some of the support we need to change.

When I was almost seventeen my pastor's wife, Mrs. Nance, asked me to be a GA leader in my home association of Baptist churches (GA stood for Girls' Auxiliary then; the organization for teenager is known as Acteens today) where she served as Woman's Missionary Union Youth director. I remember the associational GA meeting in Jonesboro, Illinois, in the back corner of the church auditorium where she talked to me about assuming this responsibility, explaining to me what would be expected. My heart pounded. My palms got sweaty. I felt scared. This was the very first time an adult had asked me to assume a formal leadership role. I had been appointed and elected to office by my peers but this was something new. It was so new, in fact, the thought had never entered my mind.

Six of us from my church had gone to the meeting in Jonesboro. As we drove home in the dark of night, I was seated in the front seat next to the door opposite the driver. I sat in silence most of the journey, overwhelmed by the mix of thoughts and feelings surging through me—happy, scared, eager, hesitant, believing, disbelieving, willing, unsure.

My church YWA (Young Woman's Auxiliary then; Baptist Young Women now) leader, Dorothy Lou, was in the seat just behind me. She was aware of what had happened, though I didn't know she was. It was such a simple thing she did. She leaned forward, reaching between the seat and the door to locate my hand. Then she squeezed my hand gently and whispered in my ear, "I think you can do it!" Her awareness, sensitivity, and support sent a surge of emotion through me. I thought I would burst containing it.

And I did do it—with God's help and the help of a lot of the people in my church. Dorothy Lou and Wayne, her husband, stood by me as Youth workers in my church. Mrs. Nance was my leader and guide. The Haussers helped me use an old mimeograph machine in their basement to put out a newsletter. My parents were always there to help. God used this experience to affirm his call to me to join him in his work in the world.

Just before Mrs. Nance died, she sent me a package of mementos she had lovingly collected—one copy of every newsletter, program folder, and so forth I led in developing as GA leader. What a gift! In opening that package, and in other strategic moments of leadership in my lifetime, I have heard Dorothy Lou's words echoing in my memory, reinforced by the support of others through the years.

I believe you can do it.

This type of experience has been repeated over and over again in my life in one form or another, as it has in yours. At change points in my life, people have been near to lend their support and guidance.

I have three letters I treasure in a special way. They were written to me by my college BSU director whom I respected and loved, by a dear friend, and by my father (one of only two or three letters I have ever received from him). These letters came at a point in my life when I was having trouble following through on a decision I had made to answer God's call to church-related service. I was enjoying teaching, and I was enjoying the financial security of my first regular job after college. For two years straight I was admitted for study at Southwestern Baptist Theological Seminary and for two years straight I decided not to go at the last minute. Two of the letters I cherish were very confrontive—challenging my indecisiveness and calling on me to make a firm decision I could implement. These letters helped me immensely, though they were not what I wanted to hear. My father's letter affirmed my decision when I was finally ready to implement it, and his letter was the most intimate statement he had ever made to me about my life—and his. My father said:

I am real glad you made the decision because I have had some decisions to make in my own life time. I felt that you were the one to make it, not myself or mother. We've been praying for you. . . . If you have made up your mind to pay the price, it will not be too hard. . . . Sometimes we must give up a good thing for the best. . . . When snow was falling, when there was no coal to heat our home, and when there was no income, my mother used to say to us, "Where there is a will, there is a way." I think you have some of that blood in you. It is no disgrace to have to manage carefully to get to do something important.

There was a ring of authenticity in my father's letter. The home he and Mother provided for us was well above average in our small town in Southern Illinois. I had never wanted for anything. It was not likely I would in the future. But, somehow giving up the known security of job and friends for the unknowns of a new career was awesome.

I knew my father could understand this. He had walked into the unknown over and over again, changing and growing. As a young boy, after his father died and because he was the oldest boy in a family of six children, he went to work to support the family. The fact that his formal education got interrupted after the eighth grade did not stop his learning. He completed a course in Complete Steam Engineering by mail later in life. At age thirty-nine, he answered a call from God to preach. He organized and pastored several churches in nearby towns while he served as chief results engineer, and later as assistant superintendent of the power plant in our hometown. Only recently have we learned the proper title for what my father did in my growing up years. He was a bivocational pastor, a type of minister only recently given a title to designate the uniqueness of the role. My father walked into many new conditions in life. When his letter came, I intuitively felt his support for me in change; today I understand his support at a much deeper level.

Support for changing cannot always come in the form of agreement and unfettered encouragement. Sometimes support comes in the form of a question, a challenge, a disagreement, a reprimand—or even from punishment. Parents do this for children, my friends did it for me in the letters they wrote challenging my indecision, supervisors must do it for employees.

At one time I served as dean of student affairs at The Southern Baptist Theological Seminary. When I took the position, it was a newly defined one, one of four major divisions of work in the seminary. One of the discussions President McCall and I had was about where responsibility for student discipline processes should be located. He asked me, "Where do you think this responsibility should be placed?"

I answered quickly, "In the Student Affairs Division." My answer was not rooted in my eagerness to handle discipline, but in my realistic assessment that supporting students in their educational pursuits meant not only the warm and caring support of them in admissions, orientation, health care, housing, student government, recreation, financial aid, chapel worship, and counseling but also the warm and caring support of them in all the crises of campus life, including any tough moments when formal discipline was required. As any parent knows, discipline is as valid an avenue of expressing love and care as serving meals and playing games together.

Most of us find it difficult to give and receive support which must come in the form of negative feedback about what we are doing. I remember with love and appreciation a colleague who said to me, "Elaine, you have very strong conceptual skills. You think fast. You reach conclusions quickly. Sometimes this has a negative impact on me and others in a group working with you. Once you work through things in your head, you sometimes show impatience with others who are still trying to get through the process leading to decision. This occasionally creates resentment toward you." Hearing this was utterly painful at first. I wanted to ignore it, deny it—anything but own up to it. Who likes to be confronted with shortcomings? But this information helped me change for the better; and I still have room to change some more.

At two different times in my career, I have experienced diminished opportunity in a job I held—some degree of failure in what I was doing. At both of these times, I could have benefited from specific feedback about what was wrong so I could change for the better. The information was unavailable or obscure. Key people who could have helped me understand what was happening only gave me vague clues. I felt a kind of blanket rejection. It has taken me years to sort out and understand what someone could have explained to me in love, if the person had had the courage.

To change and to feel supported in changing requires what a former pastor of mine calls "tough love—love that neither abandons us in indifference nor devastates us by total condemnation."[2] Tough love is Godlike. Perhaps that explains why we give and receive too little of it as human beings.

He and I happened to meet face-to-face in the busy foyer of a meeting of the Southern Baptist Convention. He called out "Dr. Dickson" and his name flashed in my mind as one of the many students I had worked with at The Southern Baptist Theological Seminary. We both reached for a handshake which turned into a hug.

It could have been an awkward moment, but it wasn't. My last personal contact with this young man was during a discipline case I had handled as dean of student affairs at the seminary. He was accused of cheating on an exam—a serious offense in any educational setting but a particularly disturbing one on a seminary campus where persons are being trained as Christian ministers.

The discipline case was a painful experience for him, for me, for the accusers, and for the Discipline Council where fellow students sat with school administrators as "the jury." As dean I managed the discipline process, trying to be as senstive as I could to the best interests of both the student and the institution. I believed the case was handled well; but, as usual, there were leftover questions about what really happened to the student in the process.

After almost ten years, the former student and I were face-to-face again. The greeting was warm. The eagerness to stop and talk seemed genuine. Then the young man said, "There are some things I want very much to say to you. I'm glad you remember me!"

"Yes," I said as I called his name.

He proceeded to tell me about himself and the church he had served as pastor since leaving the seminary. He showed healthy signs of maturing as a Christian and as a Christian minister. Listening to him brought me an overwhelming sense of gratitude that our lives had touched deeply—even in painful moments of crises.

Then he brought up the difficult subject of the discipline case. He said, "You don't know how many times I've intended to write you and didn't. I've needed you to know that the discipline experience was a turning point in my life. I know now that I was struggling with my call as a minister. I've even wondered if my careless slip into cheating was a way of having someone make a decision for me, by shutting the door to further preparation for ministry. I'm not sure about all that was going on with me then. But what I need you to know is I was able to accept help from you and others, and I was able to accept God's forgiveness. That experience made me know how vulnerable I am to doing wrong. It made me more sensitive to the hurts, struggles, and vulnerability of people with whom I minister. Thank you for the way you worked with me in that situation. Good came out of this for me—and I love and appreciate you more than I ever could have if we had not gone through this together." He hugged me again and left. Tough love.

God created us for relationships. In his wisdom, he gave us family and church, settings in which we can be nurtured and disciplined as we change and grow. In these settings—and in broader ones—he reveals to us the beautiful possibility of tough love.

This love . . . is slow to lose patience—it looks for a way of being constructive. It is not possessive: it is neither anxious to impress nor does it cherish inflated ideas of its own importance. Love has good manners and does not pursue selfish advantage. It is not touchy. It does not keep account of evil or gloat over the wickedness of other people. On the contrary, it shares the joy of those who live by the truth. Love knows no limit to its endurance, no end to its trust, no fading of its hope; it can outlast anything. Love never fails (Cor. 13:4-8, Phillips).

Support for changing comes in accepting tough love from God and from others—love which neither abandons us in indifference nor devastates us in total condemnation. Help is available if we are open to it—not tomorrow, but today. Not next year, but this year. Not after all our change is past, but in the middle of it. Not in another place, but right here where we live[3]

For some, saying no and yes to change is one endless burden; for others it is a call to joy!

For Your Reflection

1. Reflect on a major change in your life in the past. What costs did you pay in making this change? Who were the persons who supported you in the change process?

2. List the roles you occupy in life and list them (i.e., Sunday School teacher, supervisor, father, wife, PTA president). State the basic purpose you are trying to accomplish in each of these roles. Try to state your purpose in each role so it takes into account the expectations of others, as well as your expectations of yourself. What are some of the change goals you may need to set to help you more effectively fulfill your purpose?

3. What do you think about the concept of "tough love" expressed on pages 138-140? To whom are you giving this kind of love? From whom are you receiving it?

Notes

CHAPTER 1

1. Billie Pate. Introductory prayers are new or adapted material used by permission of the author or Broadman Press. Books of poetry published by Broadman Press include: *Rags, Tags, and Gentle Tears; Touch Life;* and *New Beginnings* (with Norman Bowman).

CHAPTER 2

1. Edward B. Lindaman, *Thinking in the Future Tense* (Nashville: Broadman Press, 1978) p. v.
2. This idea came from Edward B. Lindaman in a training session in Nashville, Tennessee, 1979.
3. Robert Oppenheimer. Quoted in Don Faben, *The Dynamics of Change* (New Jersey: Prentice-Hall, 1968) p. 2.
4. Richard Beckhard "OD Consulting with Dick Beckhard," Notes from a Professional Training Program in Organization Development, NTL Institute for Applied Behavioral Science, Bethel, Maine, 1971.

CHAPTER 3

1. Earl A. Loomis, *The Self in Pilgrimage* (New York: Harper and Row, 1960), p.122.
2. Kurt Lewin, *Field Theory in Social Science: Selected Theoretical Papers*, ed. Dorwin Cartwright (New York: Harper and Row, 1951).
3. Ronald Lippitt, Jeanne Watson, and Bruce Westley, *The Dynamics*

of *Planned Change* (New York: Harcourt, Brace and World, Inc., 1958), pp. 72-86.

4. Kahlil Gibran, *The Prophet* (New York: Alfred A. Knopf, 1946), p. 32. Used by permission.

5. Lippitt, Watson, and Westley, pp. 86-89.

6. The technical name for this technique is Force Field Analysis. See Lewin, pp.202-207.

CHAPTER 4

1. The author first heard Thomas R. Bennett III use this definition in a training session at Yokefellow Institute, Earlham, Indiana, 1970.

2. Herbert C. Kelman, "Process of Opinion Change," *The Planning of Change: Readings in the Applied Behavioral Sciences*, eds. Warren G. Bennis, Kenneth D. Benne, and Robert Chin (New York: Holt, Rinehart and Winston, Inc., 1961, pp. 509-517.

3. Howard P. Colson and Raymond M. Rigdon, *Understanding Your Church's Curriculum* (Nashville: Broadman Press, 1969), pp. 54-57.

4. Ibid.

5. W. T. Conner, *The Faith of the New Testamant* (Nashville: Broadman Press, 1940), p. 466.

6. Edgar H. Schein, "The Mechanisms of Change," *The Planning of Change*, 2nd ed., eds. Warren G. Bennis, Kenneth D. Benne, and Robert Chin (New York : Holt Rinehart and Winston, Inc., 1969), p. 98.

7. Baptist Press News Release, August, 1981.

8. Billie McMurry Emmons, *Letters from Mother* (Nashville: Broadman Press, 1967), p.14.

9. Ibid., pp. 14-15.

10. From T. B. Maston.

11. Joseph D. Ban, *Education for Change* (Valley Forge : Judson Press, 1968), p.60.

12. Quotation is by Billie Pate, from a poster published by Broadman Press.

13. Lindaman, pp. 5-6.

14. Quoted in Ban, pp.59-60. Oratorio by Samuel Miller.

CHAPTER 5

1. Some of these key ideas originally came from Goodman Waston, *Concepts for Social Change* (Washington: National Training Laboratories, National Education Association,1967), pp. 10-25.

2. John Gardner, *Self-Renewal: The Individual and the Innovative Society* (New York: Harper and Row, 1963), p. 126.

CHAPTER 6

1. The author's early thinking about conflict was influenced by Thomas R. Bennett III at a training session at Yokefellow Institute, Earlham, Indiana, 1969.

CHAPTER 7

1. Wayne E. Oates, in a lecture to Baptist Book Store Managers, Baptist Sunday School Board, Nashville, Tennessee, 1980.
2. John Claypool, author's pastor at Crescent Hill Baptist Church, Louisville, Kentucky in the early 1970s.
3. Adapted from Henri J. M. Nouwen, *The Wounded Healer: Ministry in Contemporary Society* (Garden City: Doubleday and Company, Inc., Image Books edition, 1979), p. 95.